C0-AUO-359

INTENTION *In Law and Society*

Also by James Marshall:

Law and Psychology in Conflict
Swords and Symbols: The Technique of Sovereignty

INTENTION—

In Law and Society

by James Marshall

Foreword by
Justice William O. Douglas

FUNK & WAGNALLS *New York*

Library of Congress Catalog Card Number: 68–12004
Published by Funk & Wagnalls, *A Division of* Reader's Digest Books, Inc.
The author is grateful for permission to reprint (on p. 180) a stanza from "The Laws of God, the laws of Man" from *The Collected Poems of A. E. Housman.* Copyright 1922 by Holt, Rinehart and Winston. Copyright 1950 by Barclays Bank Ltd. Reprinted by permission of Holt, Rinehart and Winston, Inc.
Printed in the United States of America

To the Memory of My Parents,
Louis and Florence Marshall,
And My Friend Arthur R. (Bob) Cohen

ACKNOWLEDGMENTS

The author acknowledges with thanks the comments and encouragement of the following, who have read the whole or parts of this book: Professors Hadley Cantril, Helge Mansson, Sheldon Glueck, Harold D. Lasswell, Irving Sarnoff, Alan M. Dershowitz, Alfred Cohn, Henry H. Foster, Jr., and Dr. Louis J. Soffer; the author's colleagues Ezra G. Levin and Seymour Spolter; and the help of Miriam Simons Frank for typing the manuscript.

Contents

"The thought of man shall not be tried, for the devil himself knoweth not the thought of man."

—C. J. BRIAN in Y.B. 7 Edw. IV f. 2 (Pasch. pl. 2)

Foreword

Our Puritan roots have greatly conditioned our attitudes and at times did so in ways of which we are hardly conscious. The wilderness in Biblical settings was usually a place to fear and to abhor, a place full of dangers and of evil. Our ancestors who came here therefore undertook to level the wilderness of this continent with an almost messianic fervor. That attitude plagues every conservation cause even to this day.

It was heretical to think of man in the Hindu and Buddhist sense as a member of a vast community owing respect to all other members, be they birds or animals. Man, being peculiarly gifted and endowed, was the King of all and therefore entitled to appropriate all other life to his ends, even to the point of extermination. That attitude also plagues many modern conservation causes.

To the Puritan conscience, poverty could be sinful, for if one is diligent, frugal, and long suffering, the Lord will provide. Yet we know that depressions create unemployment and technology the disemployable.

Wrongdoers are those who chose not to be good. Free will, largely though not exclusively a product of Judeo-Christian philosophy, gives every man the choice. Those who choose to be bad, who become outlaws, who commit crimes, must be punished. And so they are executed or sent to prison. Yet we now know from new disciplines that the question is often not a moral one but reducible to a tangle of imponderables beyond the control of the individual. Now a prison is the end of the road. Putting an offender there keeps him and his problems out of our consciousness. Therapy is not available, for the culprit is sinful, not sick; and prison personnel commonly play the punitive role of acting out their own hostile drives on people who are their captives. In one Southern state the qualification for the office of Superintendent of Prisons was that he loved "to whip niggers."

There is an old Jewish saying, "Build schools and centers of learning in order to safeguard the Law from becoming the property of a select group."

The Law, at any one point in time, expresses a consensus that accommodates or serves the basic interests of the Establishment. It therefore commonly has a bias against a minority, *e.g.*, the poor in this country, the dissenter in Russia, the "vagrant" both here and in Russia, and so on. It will have many another bias. In Afghanistan, at least until recently, an accused was deemed insane if he did not know the difference between the sky and the earth. In this country he is in most jurisdictions insane if he does not know right from wrong. That leaves in the outer darkness a multitude of psychopaths and others who may "know" right from wrong but who, in the totality of their makeups, feel no compunctions of guilt when they cross the line, or those who are sick as a result of unknown imponderables which may even cause a chemical imbalance in their systems. Their plight is compounded by reason of the fact that those who sit in judgment on them—juries and judges—are largely ignorant of mental illness or have one of their own which makes them unsympathetic arbiters; moreover, under most regimes they are deprived by rules of law of such enlightenment as a specialist could give them. As I say, when the accused is shipped off to prison, the case is at an end, for the prejudice or ignorance that sent him there does not supply the therapy that we have reason to believe might be amazingly successful in 50 per cent of the cases; and the results would be startling if we endowed the project with the same energy, fervor, and resources that we expend in Vietnam.

But our growing insight into the problems of mental health has not as yet had much of an impact on the law, which means that it is still "the property of a select group" dominated by the Puritan ethic.

I have mentioned only a few of the nests that the present volume disturbs. It is provocative and I hope disturbing, for only by keeping the noses of the powers-that-be close to these problems can we hope to lessen at home man's inhumanity to his neighbor.

William O. Douglas

INTENTION [1]: *In Law and Society*

Introduction

IN LAW the concept of intent is frequently a critical factor. In more serious crimes the evil intention of the defendant is an element of the crime and may determine the penalty inflicted on a guilty party.* It is an element of some torts, that is, civil wrongs committed against persons or their property, such as fraud, malicious mischief, assault and battery, libel and slander. Intention is involved in the interpretation of wills and contracts. It is a fact that must be shown and found in litigation in those areas of law. It is principally with intent as a factor in determining *legal culpability* that this book is concerned.

What does intent or intention mean in law? Is it the same in relation to crimes and the tort of deceit as in the interpretation of documents, i.e., legislation, contracts, deeds, and wills? What does psychology mean by intent; in other words, how do psychologists describe the phenomenon? To what extent does psychology support the legal description and how do

* Congress "has seen fit to prescribe that an evil state of mind, described variously in one or more such terms as 'intentional,' 'wilful,' 'knowing,' 'fraudulent' or 'malicious,' will make criminal an otherwise indifferent act, or increase the degree of the offense or its punishment."[1] [Superscript numerals refer to notes, which will be found in a separate section following the text.]

they conflict? What legal "make believe" is contained in the legal concept of intent? Is this "make believe" misleading and does it conflict with the purposes of law? If so, how can legal doctrine and procedures be modified to conform better to psychological phenomena?

The problem of intent raises further questions. How does someone performing an act perceive his own intentions? How does an observer of his behavior, a witness, perceive them? How do judge and jury, the triers of fact, perceive the intention of the actor and reach a conclusion based on their percep-ions?

Meaning of Intention in Law

Empirically we know little about intention. The psychologist cannot trust a person's declaration as to what his own intentions are or what they have been. [The lawyer accepts a defendant's version of his intentions when the law assumes the declaration to be against the declarant's interest, i.e., as when he admits an evil intent; but the lawyer is not as ready to believe a person's denial, i.e., as when he makes a statement in his own interest.] The best that the psychologist can do is to apply empirical knowledge of related psychological states to the problem of intention. The lawyer is satisfied with a priori reasoning and dialectics.[2] This becomes apparent when one considers definitions of intent.

In criminal law the courts, in order to meet the problem of intent in different situations,

> *have devised working formulae*, if not scientific ones, for the instruction of juries around such terms as "felonious intent," "criminal intent," "malice aforethought," "guilty knowledge," "fraudu-

lent intent," "wilfulness," "*scienter*," to denote guilty knowledge, or "*mens rea*," to signify an evil purpose or mental culpability. By use or combination of these various tokens, they have sought to protect those who were not blameworthy in mind from conviction of infamous common-law crimes.[3]

If lawyers "have devised working formulae," what of psychologists? They are less likely to use the term *intent*. They may speak of *motivation*, for example, and to meet their needs devise such concepts as "drives," "motives," "needs," "goal-seeking behavior," etc.[4] The varied terminology in law and psychology should alert us to our uncertainty as to those psychological phenomena which we invoke to determine guilt.

Are these "working formulae" (so variously devised to guide laymen to judge whether an act was intentionally performed and whether that intention was evil) necessary because lawyers have been unable to settle in their own minds the nature of intent? It would certainly appear that they do not trust the lay mind of the juror. Most laymen would probably accept the definition of the Concise Oxford Dictionary[5] that a person does something with intent when he does it "on purpose." The great Oxford dictionary edited by Murray expresses the same concept. Intent, it says, is "The act or fact of intending or *purposing;* intention, purpose (*formed in the mind*). . . . Now chiefly in legal phraseology, and in the expressions *with intent to* (*hurt, etc.*), *with good or malicious intent, etc.*"[6] And again, "what is in the mind, notion, or thought of any kind."[7]

Thus, added to purpose is the concept that intent is in the mind, which has presented problems to law and psychology, and the further element of malicious intent or *mens rea* in criminal offenses.

Mens rea comes to us through the old legal maxim

Actus non facit reum, nisi mens sit rea. An act does not make [the doer of it] guilty, unless the mind be guilty; that is, unless the intention be criminal. . . . The intent and the act must both concur to constitute the crime.[8]

Bouvier in discussing *mens rea* quotes this definition:

To an unlegal mind, it suggests that, by the law of England, no act is a crime which is done from laudable motives; in other words, that immorality is essential to crime.[9]

Black gives us another extension of the legal definition of intent:

When used with reference to civil and criminal responsibility, a person who contemplates any result, as not unlikely to follow from a deliberate act of his own, may be said to intend that result, whether he desire it or not . . . Mozley & Whitley.[10]

In other words, a reckless act may be treated *As If* it resulted from a malicious purpose. So a man who shoots a gun in a crowded place and kills another may be held guilty of murder, as would one who plots the death of another, lies in wait, and shoots him, though perhaps to a lesser degree. For in either case death of another would not be unlikely to follow the deliberate act of shooting. From this follows the principle that if someone is killed in the course of commission of another felony (a bank robbery, for example) all who are engaged in the felony are guilty of murder. The dialectic which stretches the legal mind to encompass an accomplice who may not even have been present when the killing occurred certainly stretches the intending mind of the accomplice.[11]

Courts have sought to distinguish between intent and motive. Although it has been said that "intent often exists where motive is wanting," it has more frequently been stated that motive is the "object," "spring," "inducement," "desire," or "moving power," whereas intent is the "object of an act," "the purpose or design" involving the will.[12]

Wigmore distinguishes *intent* from *knowledge* and *design.* He tells us that "*Intent* involves often nothing more than knowledge or hostile feeling" and that "if knowledge or hostile feeling (malice) can be shown specifically, there may be inferred immediately the criminal intent. . . . But Intent more frequently signifies (*ante*) merely the absence of accident, inadvertence, or casualty,—a varying state of mind which is the contrary of an innocent state of mind. . . ." [13] This means that if there be no evidence of "accident, inadvertence, or casualty" the law will treat an act *As If* there were a criminal intent; and that without more ado intent can be found from the mere existence of knowledge or hostile feeling, that is, malice.

Psychologists are not so clear that these distinctions are valid. For example, Cantril says that intention develops "to satisfy feeling favorable to the well-being of the organism" and that without this "there is no attention." He cites the neurologist Ralph Gerard. Gerard describes the manner in which nerve impulses were received and stored as memories or information. Overt behavior, he said, "which is not immediately related to any input" could flow "from this rich central store. . . . *Such separation in time and type (and locus) of stimulus and response gives the richness and spontaneity of behavior experienced as volition and rationalized as free will.*" [emphasis added][14] In other words, each individual has a great many perceptions stored within the nervous system, and from this "rich central store" he selects, usually unconsciously, an appropriate response to a given situation. The combinations and interactions involved in this selection which determine his response are a function of his unique personality makeup and the situation. Thus calling appropriate responses from his experience, perhaps derived from different situations, he is not limited to automatic behavior. In this sense the individual can be said to have made a voluntary choice.

To Gerard both "behaviorism" and "uncaused cause" were unacceptable. "Whatever the degree of contingency at each level or organization, there is no place for a directed random event, and a general chain exists—of causality down levels and of purpose up them." [15]

The relationship of intention to attention, purpose, and motivational meaning stressed by Cantril is illustrated in the Hebrew word *kavanah*. *Kavanah* is used for "meaning, purpose, motive, and intention" and refers to "the direction of the mind towards the accomplishment of a particular act, the state of being aware of what we are doing, of the task we are engaged in" and thus really means *attentiveness*.[16]

A crime committed with intent involves not only *mens rea*, the evil mind, but also *actus reus*, the evil deed, the evil hand. But *actus reus* may of itself be criminal when it is an unlawful act performed *maliciously, knowingly*. This distinction is illustrated by the case of Regina v. Charlson.[17] The defendant struck his son with a mallet and threw him out of the window. The boy was not killed. There were three charges: "causing grievous bodily harm" (1) "with intent to murder" the boy; (2) "with the intention of causing him some grievous bodily harm"; and (3) "without any specific allegation as to his intention." [18] As to the first two charges, the court instructed the jury that the prosecutor must prove intent. With respect to the third count, the question was whether the act was one of automatism or was maliciously done, in which case the act must have been performed with knowledge by the defendant of what he was doing and that it was unlawful. The judge charged:

> Lastly, there is *the third charge* of inflicting grievous bodily harm. In relation to that charge the prosecution *need not prove a definite intent*. They do *have to* prove, however, that the *grievous bodily harm* was caused by the accused *unlawfully and maliciously*. *This means* that there *must be a conscious* act on the part of the accused. Malice does not necessarily involve the existence of some hostility to the person injured. It does, however, mean that the act must be done consciously. In order to commit an unlawful and malicious act, the accused must know what he is doing and must realize that he has no lawful justification for his act.[19] [emphasis added]

This is an illustration of Wigmore's distinction between intent and knowledge.

Holmes, in that astoundingly modern volume published in 1881, *The Common Law*, tells us that

> Malice, as used in common speech, includes intent, and something more. When an act is said to be done with an intent to do harm, it is meant that a wish for the harm is the motive of the act. *Intent, however, is perfectly consistent with the harm being regretted as such, and being wished only as a means to something else*. But when an act is said to be done maliciously, it is meant, not only that a wish for the harmful effect is the motive, but also that the harm is wished for its own sake, or, as Austin would say with more accuracy, for the sake of the pleasurable feeling which knowledge of the suffering caused by the act would excite.[20] [emphasis added]

Furthermore, he points out that

> It is just as much murder to shoot a sentry for the purpose of releasing a friend, as to shoot him because you hate him. Malice . . .

in view of the considerations just mentioned, . . . has been thought to mean criminal intention.

But intent again will be found to resolve itself into two things; foresight that certain consequences will follow from an act, and the wish for those consequences working as a motive which induces the act. The question then is, whether intent, in its turn, cannot be reduced to a lower term. Sir James Stephen's statement shows that it can be, and that knowledge that the act will probably cause death, that is, foresight of the consequences of the act, is enough in murder as in tort.[21]

Generally crime is only present when there is a "concurrence of an evil-meaning mind with an evil-doing hand," and this concept "was congenial to an intense individualism and took deep and early root in American soil." [22]

Mr. Justice Jackson cites from Radin to the effect that "determination of the boundary between intent and negligence spells freedom or condemnation. . . ." [23] A penal system that neglects the mental element will not be generally acceptable because popularly intention and freedom of will are believed to be axiomatic.[24] Furthermore, according to Sayre, it would outrage popular feeling to punish severely a morally innocent person who brought about an injury through reasonable mistake or accident.[25]

Thus we find moral values implicit in our definition of crime and evil intent used as the norm by which to satisfy the need for a moral solution of the problem of guilt. We see too that intent is treated as a purpose formed in the mind to do something maliciously or reckless of consequences, not accidentally.*

Recent literature in social psychology and sociology sug-

* We are not now considering those offenses not arising out of the common law, which require no proof of intent.[26]

gests considerable gaps between legal theory and the realities of human life. Both law and the social sciences in general base findings of intent and purpose on probabilities. Law tends to direct its attention to the probable intent of *men* even when the probable intent of a given *man* is at issue. This is a derivation from the historical development of the law and the lack of reality inherent in the adversary system of trial. The fact-finding system of science is, of course, quite different. The argument of this book comes down to the question of whether scientific inquiry can and will be tried to help law adapt to changing times and knowledge.

I Background and Legal History

THAT AN INJURY is to be deemed a crime "only when inflicted by intention is no provincial or transient notion," Jackson says. "It is as universal and persistent in mature systems of law as belief in freedom of the human will and a consequent ability and duty of the normal individual to choose between good and evil." [1] But this has not always been true. Freedom of will and presumed ability to make a choice have not been the bases for determining wrongdoing in all cultures or at all times,[2] even in Anglo-American law.

Early law found itself unequal to the effort of passing judgment on the psychological elements in crime. In the late Middle Ages an English judge (Chief Justice Brian) said, "The thought of man shall not be tried, for the devil himself knoweth not the thought of man." This "might well be the motto for the early history of criminal law. It can not go behind the visible fact." [3] Intent was an internal matter and the early judges did not have the temerity to uncover it.

The same judicial humility existed in the case of conspiracy, covin. "Covin, it was said, is a secret thing contained in the heart of a man which by intendment another person can have no knowledge of." [4]

In general it was the injury, the harm, that was paid for in life or limb or property. Where no harm was done there could be no crime. Attempted crime was not punishable where there was no actual damage done.[5] In the oldest recorded cases in English law there was apparently no attempt to distinguish a situation in which the dead man could be found at fault from those instances in which he had shown no negligence or recklessness. On the other hand, one accused of an offense could not plead his own negligence or lack of intention to do harm, for he had in fact "hurt the plaintiff's body." [6] But the instrument of an injury was frequently forfeited, and Pollock and Maitland tell us that the large number of deodands collected (gifts to God, accepted by the Crown in His name) "suggests that many horses and boats bore the guilt which should have been ascribed to beer. A drunken carter is crushed beneath the wheel of his cart; the cart, the cask of wine that was in it and the oxen that were drawing it are all deodand."

Not only was a man responsible for harm which resulted from his own acts but also from the acts of his slaves and beasts and other personal property. "If his sword kills, he will have great difficulty in swearing that he did nothing whereby the dead man was 'further from life or nearer to death.' " If his sword wounded someone while it was being sharpened by a smith, the owner might have to make payment to one who was injured by it. Just as the table into which the little child bumps is held guilty of the injury, so any property, whether its owner were present and using it or not, might be held guilty and become a deodand "devoted to God." [7]

This practice was not peculiar to English law. Blood feuds were reported in the Caucuses resulting from such situations as a pasturing sheep dislodging a stone which killed someone.

This was "just cause for a feud" between the family of the deceased and the owner of the sheep. Even the family of a thief who was killed if the gun he had stolen went off had "a just feud against the owner of the gun." [8] Crime was prosecuted whether by feud or in court by the injured party, not the state, and there was little or no distinction, of course, between crime and tort as we now know them.*

We are told that Jewish law "refuses to accept the principle that under all circumstances the intention determines the deed." The goodness of a good deed is not necessarily destroyed because of the absence of a right intention. "Deed and thought are bound into one. All a person thinks and feels enters into everything he does and all he does is involved in anything he thinks and feels." [10]

However, the evidence is that people regarded intentional homicide as worse than unintentional and there gradually developed the differentiation between the intentional and the nonintentional or accidental injury. Attempted crime, too, became subject to the attention of the court. It is possible that this development was the result of the growth of the king's court and a greater variety in the punishments that it could inflict. It may be, too, that with the influence of Roman law and Canon law in the development of English law in the twelfth and thirteenth centuries, concepts of greater flexibility

* "Guesswork perhaps would have taught us that barbarians will not trace the chain of causation beyond its nearest link, and that, for example, they will not impute one man's death to another unless that other has struck a blow which laid a corpse at his feet. All the evidence however points the other way:—I have slain a man if but for some act of mine he might perhaps be yet alive . . . At your request I accompany you when you are about your own affairs; my enemies fall upon and kill me; you must pay for my death. You take me to see a wild-beast-show or that interesting spectacle a madman; beast or madman kills me; you must pay. You hang up your sword; some one else knocks it down so that it cuts me; you must pay. In none of these cases can you honestly swear that you did nothing that helped to bring about death or wound." [9]

were available. Certainly the Canon law had many degrees of guilt related to a scale of punishments, from life imprisonment to disqualifying a clerk from further promotion. No such variety existed in early English law. There is evidence that the law fluctuated and by the twelfth century "actions on the case" were being introduced with the idea that "liability should be based, not merely upon an act forbidden by the law which has damaged the plaintiff, but upon an act done negligently by the defendant." The courts were also commencing to consider abandoning the view "that it was impossible to base civil liability upon intention to deceive, because it was impossible to try the thought of man." [11]

We learn from history, early literature, and modern anthropology that crime, proof, and legal sanctions were related to religious belief.* Early forms of proof, whether ordeals or oaths, "were appeals to the supernatural." In many lands the red-hot iron and the pond were used to demonstrate guilt or innocence. In Western Europe in the Middle Ages the Church ritualized ordeals inherited from the barbarians. The oath, by which the witness submitted himself to divine punishment had he sworn falsely, was part of the ordeal.[13] The vestigial remnant of this oath which is no longer an "assertory oath," but promissory, still concludes in our courts with "So help me God."

When men and women were burned at the stake their souls were consigned, possibly to the mercy, but more probably, judging by the prevalent circumstances, to the punishing wrath, of God. And the deodand (gift to God), already noted as a sanction of the law, consisting of any property which was

* It has been suggested that some of the fictions and rituals of modern law come to us from ancient magic predating the periods of classical Greece and Rome.[12]

instrumental in causing death, was forfeited to the Crown acting as God's surrogate.*

Primitive peoples in many parts of the world assigned a man's soul or his strength to his hair, believing that if his hair were cut he would die or grow weak.† (This was magic to them; they had no Freud to diagnose their castration complex.) It was the custom in Europe in medieval times to shave the whole bodies of sorcerers to destroy their power. The threat to cut the hair of the accused or a witness has been used, even in modern times, by colonial governments to obtain confessions. And it would seem that depilitation has frequently served as the "third degree" does today.[15]

Among the Ashanti, if no intent could be established, or a killing could be shown to have been accidental, it "would be accepted as the action of an evil spirit misdirecting the activities of the killer." [16] We, who relegate to "acts of God" those phenomena we cannot attribute to human beings, should not ridicule primitive societies which find answers in the action of evil or avenging spirits.‡

* "The deodand may warn us that in ancient criminal law there was a sacral element which Christianity could not wholly suppress, especially when what might otherwise have been esteemed a heathenry was in harmony with some of those strange old dooms that lie embedded in the holy books of the Christian. Also it is hard for us to acquit ancient law of that unreasoning instinct that impels the civilized man to kick, or consign to eternal perdition, the chair over which he has stumbled. *But law which would not confess to sanctioning this instinct still finds grave difficulties in its way if it endeavors to detect and appreciate the psychical element in guilt and innocence*" [14] [emphasis added].

† The Old Testament has many references to people cutting their hair to expiate offenses. Note too the story of Samson and Delilah.

‡ Accidental killing was excused by the Barama River Carib because "The Carib philosophy on the matter of intent, stated in our terms, follows the reasoning that accidents are to be classed along with that whole group of natural incidents which are often injurious and inconvenient to human beings. The causes, however, are spiritual or supernatural, and the results are due to transgression, perhaps unconscious, of a tabu. If a man kills or poisons another by accident, he is merely acting as unconscious agent of the spiritual powers who constitute the effective agent and cannot be punished." [17]

Intention to commit a homicide was a criminal act treated by the Ashanti as no less heinous than murder. They classified it as *awudie* [i.e., heinous]. Evidence was to be found in certain acts or words which the defendant may have performed or uttered—"I shall not eat again"—holding a knife at right angles in cutting an object—letting his hair grow long if he was not a priest or about to go into battle.[18]

We should not scoff at the ritual character of Ashanti evidence, for perhaps they would do the same with regard to some of ours. It is possible, moreover, that the intending murderer might be subconsciously compelled to perform one or more of the ritual acts to express his guilt, just as with us the criminal may be unconsciously impelled at times to set the cues to his own discovery.

The divine origin of law was the recognized doctrine of political and religious philosophers and legal writers during the centuries in which Roman, Canon, and common law developed. There was one law, "eternal and immutable," according to Cicero, embracing "all peoples for all time" and as it were "one common master and ruler, the god of all, the author and judge and proposer of this law." [19]

To the people of the Middle Ages, law was the "gift and invention of God," and, said Hooker, "Of the law there can be no less acknowledged, than that her seat is the bosom of God, her voice the harmony of the world." [20]

St. Thomas Aquinas taught that through "the illumination of God" men know the principles of natural law and have "a natural inclination to observe them." This does not apply to human laws, however, which cannot become known intuitively. According to St. Thomas, a ruler "had a primary responsibility to God, who was the author of the law upon which the ruler's authority rested." [21]

After the reign of Stephen in the twelfth century, there was increasing contact between English law and Roman and Canon law. Large parts of the law of England were turned over to ecclesiastical courts and this, too, resulted in the thought and practices of Canon law affecting the judges and legal writers at the time in which the common law was developing.[22] Church courts made broad claims to jurisdiction "to correct the sinner for his soul's health," which the king's court resisted "by asserting that, if the sin be also an offense which they can punish, the spiritual judges are not to meddle with it." [23] Nevertheless the Church courts took over for the most part sexual crimes—fornication, adultery, incest—and defamation of character (though the local courts had jurisdiction of libel and slander) and usury, perjury for the most part, and, of course, simony.[24] The Church also claimed jurisdiction of wills, for the last testament was deemed to be connected with the last confession and "a notion prevailed that intestacy, if it be not exactly a sin, is often God's judgment on sin" and that "to die intestate is to die unconfessed." [25]

Historically law and crime were related to religious belief and Church doctrine, so it is not surprising that serious crimes should be associated with wickedness and sinfulness. The very words used to describe felonious crimes and intent to commit them demonstrate this sense of wickedness and sinfulness in which we and our ancestors have held them. Felony was infamous, "as bad a word as you can give a man or thing." [26] Perhaps, as Coke suggested, it comes from the Latin word for gall, "the original sense being one who is full of bitterness or venom." [27] Here we see the early association of serious crime with the bitter, poisonous, hostile person, one who intends evil, possessed of *mens rea*. In English law "felon" first appears to stand for cruel, fierce, wicked, base, although sometimes admiringly for fierceness and courage. It becomes associated with malice aforethought and malice prepense.

Free Will

As has been shown, the English common law grew up without the concept of criminal intent as an element of a crime. It tried "to make men answer for all the ills of an obvious kind that their deeds bring upon their fellows." [28] Many statutory crimes require no proof of intent.[29] Common-law felonies, however, are and have been regarded as heinous because men believe them to have been purposively done.

Moreover as common law developed the felon was seen as rejecting the law which emanated from God. The sinner chose to sin. In Western culture the authority of sacred writings emphasized the sinfulness of crimes which other societies also condemned but did not necessarily regard as sinful. The Ten Commandments, among other imperatives, forbid theft, adultery, murder, and bearing false witness. But according to Deuteronomy (probably the earliest written book of the Bible), man had the choice of observing or violating Biblical law.

> See, I have set before thee this day life and good, and death and evil. . . . I call heaven and earth to witness against you this day, that I have set before thee life and death, the blessing and the curse; therefore choose life, that thou mayest live, thou and thy seed. . . .[30]

This Hebraic doctrine was at the foundation of the Church doctrine of free will. It did not conflict with Luther's doctrinal break with the Church but helped the Protestant internalization of conscience. Even Calvinist determinism could accept free will in the sphere of law, however much it insisted on preordination of salvation.

The idea of a voluntary choice between good and evil was not only derived from the Judeo-Christian tradition. This was reinforced by Aristotle, known to lawyers from the teachings of the late medieval universities. Aristotle believed that the selection of means toward an end was a deliberative process. It was the result of a choice. It was voluntary. We could do or not do. We could say yes or we could say no, and consequently vice was voluntary. However, he said, if a man was voluntarily unjust, then it did not follow that he could rectify the situation if he wished to cease being unjust any more than a sick man can become healthy by wishing to be entirely well.[31]

As has already been suggested, the problem of free will, of choice, arose not so much in relation to proof that an injury had been done as in connection with the justification of punishment, for "unmerited punishment (to a lesser extent also undeserved reward) offends the general sense of justice." The general opinion is that severe sanctions should only be invoked when the offense is committed by choice, on purpose, and lesser sanctions as they became available to the law would be applied to instances where a man was otherwise responsible.[32]

> The reason for requiring an act is, that an act implies a choice, and that it is felt to be impolitic and unjust to make a man answerable for harm, unless he might have chosen otherwise. But the choice must be made with a chance of contemplating the consequence complained of, or else it has no bearing on responsibility for that consequence.[33]

Law, through the concept of intention, presumes that a person is responsible for his intended acts and therefore is responsible to society for those acts.* What the law does is to polarize behavior affecting others as good or evil, applying the belief system, which is so strongly stated in our Western culture, that men have free will. Out of this cultural experience we therefore perceive behavior to be good or evil—good if a man makes a socially acceptable choice, evil if he does not. Thus we tend to perceive the socially unacceptable act as one of choice and intentional wrongdoing, the result of a decision to do wrong. Most cultures, however, are less positive.

> There are not many cultures, for example, where a rigid dichotomy between good and evil, such as we have set up, is insisted upon. Rather it is recognized that good and evil are but the extremes of a continuously varied scale between these poles that produces only different degrees of greyness.[34]

The fact that absolute values of good and evil tend to be stressed in our culture makes it difficult to understand or apply a relativistic view of behavior.

When the law of England reached the point at which it distinguished between intended and unintended acts, judges and lawyers were already conditioned by the doctrine of free will. The derivations of ethical-legal values from religious doctrine almost of necessity resulted in acceptance of free will.

But do we have free will? Do we have choices, or is everything that we do predetermined in one manner or another? Quantum mechanics denies the possibility of knowing how and when any particular atom will perform.

Einstein hypothesized in his formula $E = mc^2$ that mass

* It is a confusion to equate psychological responsibility for the performance of an act with responsibility to society for the injury caused by the act. Without any intent or motive to do harm a driver may misjudge distance and cause an accident for which society will hold him liable; or a man may with intent break his dishes, be responsible for breaking them, yet not be socially responsible for the act.

and energy are interchangeable. The scientists who split the atom proved this theory. We now know the truth of it, to our disquiet. It seems probable that the age-old concept that man could land on the moon will soon be demonstrated. It is true that Einstein and the atom smashers were, and the moon landers will be, dependent on prior mathematical and scientific experience and to that extent will not be free. But these events were not or will not be inevitable, nor was it inevitable that they would occur in the twentieth century. Men had to make choices and act on those choices. Einstein had to make choices in arriving at his formula, Roosevelt to use it in making an atomic bomb, Truman to drop the bomb on Hiroshima. Choices have been and are being made concerning sending men to the moon. Without conscious choices being made and the freedom to make them, those events would not just happen. To believe otherwise, to believe that it was somehow predetermined, whether by some spiritual being or by necessity arising out of physiological or psychological compulsions in the human organism, would be to assume a world in which the behavior of man made no difference. Granted we shall die, does it make no difference in the happenings of our lives if we exert no effort to find food and shelter, no difference whether we isolate ourselves from others, find mutual support with them, or seek satisfaction through their destruction?

Granted, too, that past experience determines the present and *affects* the future, that, as Gerard said, there are no "uncaused causes." It does not contradict the existence of volition and *determine* the future. Each of us has a different past, a different set of experiences, and therefore perceptions and set toward events. They circumscribe our freedom but do not eliminate it. New situations and new pressures impose choices.

We are continually being changed through transactions with others, resulting in new internal and external tensions that need satisfaction. This frequently requires choice. To cause children to make socially acceptable choices is both a goal and achievement of education, training, and other forms of acculturation. Choice itself—through the process of resolving conflicting apparently contradictory perceptions of a situation—may result in change.[35]

Of course there are physical and psychological limits to free will. The cultural and personal past live in each individual's present and to a degree canalize his feelings and behavior.

However, greater insight into the nature of man and his environment and his interrelationship with it and increased knowledge of the causes of misbehavior "cannot in the least alter the fact *that* I will but it can alter *what* I will." [36] It can broaden my field of choice. Greater insight and knowledge can also help me judge what others will and what their motives are, what they intend, and to what extent their behavior relates to their will.

Determinism has been said to be a half-truth which "need not rob us of our conviction that we participate creatively in our own advance. As human beings we can still, within limits, ask the question: 'What do I choose to become?' " [37] Or we can inquire, "What shall I choose to do?" and having chosen attempt to do it.

Men certainly behave in the belief that they have choice and in the expectation that they and others have freedom to make choices. It is their behavior as they perceive it, "not something else which philosophers and moralists mean," [38] that is the subject of law and gives it such reality as it has as a phenomenon of social life.

But *can* we really choose, really exercise will? This is the eternal question of *free will.* We must distinguish at once between the person's *perception* that he has or has not free will, and the larger philosophical question of the existence and nonexistence of free will. Our concern here is solely with the former, which is a more limited perceptual issue.[39]

Despite the determinism of may philosophers, theologians, and scientists, we perceive ourselves engaging in voluntary actions which we perform by choice, not as automata. This may be illusory, but without this illusion we probably could not survive. Certainly our transactions with other human beings and with nature would be difficult, if not impossible, and our institutions, including law and science, could not come into being. It seems probable that the breakdown in established values and institutions today is related to our feeling of helplessness, our extremely limited feeling of choice (1) in the presence of the potential, which is in the hands of a few almost unreachable men, to destroy the race; (2) our sense of distance from power centers of political, economic, and social control; and (3) a feeling of uselessness of personal skills in the face of technological developments. Such a reduction in a sense of personal power must, as we shall see later, either arouse hostility, apathy, or denial of reality. Many of our young people try to gain a sense of social power by rejecting the cultural past and authority and find reassurance in existential philosophy. Many of them feel "alienated" because they sense helplessness in influencing important aspects of their lives.

Yet the "fiction" of freedom, if it is fiction, is strongly with us. We agonize over our choices, feel guilt if we make the "wrong" ones. We do not behave as if we were really convinced that we have no freedom. It has been said that man's only freedom really consists in his ability to make gracefully the choices that he *has* to make; but even this implies that he still exercises some real choice.[40]

In summary, it is difficult to conceive of a person having free will independent of his experience-conditioned perceptions and his transactions with other people and with objects which compose a given situation in which he interacts. It is equally difficult to accept the thesis that man has no freedom of will to mediate among his own purposes and the people, objects, and culture which compose the field of his interactions. It is not possible for man by his will to eliminate his experience and perceive people or things or interrelationships *de novo*, or, if he is not pathological, to ignore the mutuality of his transactions with others. But the experience-conditioned perceptions of an individual are never identical with those of other individuals and therefore the choices and values attached to them tend to differ; and the will to be free enough to make the choices they perceive will vary in force.

II Social Condition and Freedom of Choice

IN LAW intention is assumed to involve the making of choices.* But are all people capable of making a choice? Do they have the same choices available? Having made a cognitive choice are all people equally capable of acting upon it? The law, with a few exceptions, has assumed and still does that the answers are affirmative. The law assumes that people (infants and the "insane" excepted)† have the same choices available and equal capacity to make a choice and then act upon it. At this point law and psychology come in conflict, for psychology considers more phenomena relevant in determining whether a specific individual can make a choice and implement it, can exercise free will. It is more open to the consideration of variables, less ready to generalize than is the law.‡

The law—or perhaps it would be better to say lawyers—in

* This chapter does not consider the questions of choice involved in determining the intent or intendment of documents, nor is it concerned with problems of the unconscious and neuroses.

† For a discussion of the differences in attitude of lawyers and psychiatrists toward the nature or even existence of a condition called "insanity" and the effects of such difference on the testimony of psychiatrists, see Menninger and Statten, "What Psychiatry Proposes for Offenders." [1]

‡ This difference in approach may be the result of differences in methodology of fact finding. Furthermore, the traditional processes of the trial have not developed a readiness for reliable fact finding as to the intention and capacities for choice and action of a party to the litigation.[2]

using "the legal hypotheses of freedom of will as the foundation of guilt is [in] the habit of asking whether or not *man*, in the abstract, 'possesses freedom of will.'"[3] This may or may not be philosophically valid; but as the problem of law, as of psychology, is concerned with the guilt and degree of free will of specific men, not *man*, the philosophical concept, though relevant as historical-psychological gestalt, is not helpful. It does not follow from the assumption that *man as an abstraction* has free will that every individual man has the same choices available to him, or the capacity to choose or act on his choice in a specific situation. To hold a man liable for an intended act, regardless of the fact that psychologically or motorically he had no choice, is not very different from the more primitive concept of law that held a man responsible for every consequence of every act, as in a situation in which his companion would not have been accidentally killed had he not invited him to go walking.[4] In both situations man plus happening would be equated to causality. But causality cannot be equated to intent. While there is a relationship between the act and the result, it is improper to hypothesize that because man in the abstract has a measure of *free will* there was a *free choice* made by a specific man which resulted in a specific injury.

Glueck says that "an understandable psychologic definition of an individual's freedom of will is his particular capacity for conscious, purposive, controlled action when confronted with a series of alternatives."[5] From this concept it would follow that *freedom of will is dependent on* (1) *the capacity of a particular individual to choose his action and* (2) *the choices which he perceives to be available to him.*

To a limited extent the law recognizes this by accepting such defenses as insanity, immaturity, and self-defense, for example. But these are crude measures to deal with the subtle distinctions of capacity and perception and availability of choices among individuals. And the legal concepts of how a "reasonable man" ("foresighted man," or as the *Model Penal Code* puts it, "law-abiding person") would act, or what he should foresee, cloud the phenomenon of the individual interacting in a specific situation.

Let us look at the matter of available choices. Whose available choices are those of this make believe, reasonable man—the choices available to the legally trained judge, the upper- and lower-middle-class juror,* or the poor man? The space of movement and therefore of free choice is not the same, nor perceived to be the same by the well-to-do and those who live in poverty—those who are socially accepted and those who are rejected by society. A person's own sense of his freedom of will is in part determined by his "space of free movement." [7] This is a Lewinian term by which he meant that the individual or social group has freedom of three kinds of "locomotion" within boundaries, i.e., bodily, social, and mental locomotion. Poverty limits physical mobility; it reduces social mobility; and because it is usually a function of lack of education and opportunity to learn about other social orders or subcultures and often social institutions created for the benefit of the poor, poverty limits mental mobility. The space of free movement of the poor is less than that of the middle class.[8]

The same would be true of the sense of time. Lewin, who speaks of "life-space"—which includes not only "space of free movement" but also "time perspective"—points out that one's life-space is not limited to the present, but "includes the future, the present, and also the past. Actions, emotions, and cer-

* In the deliberations of a jury, it was found that jurors of higher social status carried the most weight.[6]

tainly the morale of an individual at any instant depend upon his total time perspective." [9] Time perspective, he points out, is relevant to a sense of reality. The infant or the young child cannot distinguish with clarity between his fantasies and external reality. His judgment is greatly dependent upon his wishes and his fears. With maturity a person is better able to separate wishes from expectations. "His life space differentiates into a 'level of reality' and various 'levels of irreality,' such as fantasy and dream." [10] Can the specific person look forward to changes in the future? Can he postpone satisfactions or does he feel that he must enjoy them now or never? On the answers to these questions depends the extent of his psychological freedom of choice, and thus his intention.

An individual's space and time perspective of free movement are related to his education, perceived opportunities available, social mobility, and to his self-perception. People of extremely low status are usually more limited than those of higher status in their sources of information and therefore their communication is more limited. They do not have the same opportunities to *develop* efficiency in judgment or the ability to reason as high-status people. Their time perspective is centered on the here and now of daily living.[11] *

The poor man, as John Adams wrote, "feels himself out of the sight of others; groping in the dark. Mankind takes no notice of him." He may not be disapproved, censured, or reproached—"he is only not seen." [12] As he sees himself and the world, will his life-space, his time-space, or his values be the

* Time and space perspectives may differ with cultures and roles. The perspective of time will not be the same in a new culture, or in a revolutionary culture, as in older cultures such as the Chinese before Mao Tse-Tung and the Jewish culture of the ghettoes. The space perspective of a medieval merchant traveling from fair to fair, or a traveler by a jet airplane, will not be similar to that of a serf or a small farmer in the Appalachian or Himalayan Mountains.

same as those of the judge and legislator? Will a reasonable man to him, i.e., in his world, be the same as a reasonable man to them, i.e., in their middle-class world?

Katherine Mansfield's pathetic story of Miss Brill illuminates the point. Miss Brill sat on a park bench feeling herself an actress in the great scene of people around her, caressing her beloved shabby little fur neckpiece with its button eyes and broken nose. She was proud of it and loved it. The miserable little fur gave her self-respect and confidence until a young girl on the bench next to her described it to her lover as "so funny," "exactly like a fried whiting." [13] Miss Brill's perception and the little fantasies on which she had built her self-esteem were constructed of the choices available to her and her values were defined by these choices, satisfying so long as mankind took no notice of her, but fragile when she was forced to relate them to the values of others.

Our experiences, the expectations and values we derive from them, our reference groups and ego-maintaining needs, will determine what we perceive. The same person may appear to different people to be well dressed or the possessor of good clothes, a "homeowner" or the possessor of a house,[14] a jolly fellow or a lazy bum, a great leader or a demagogue.

Education in Middle-Class Values

Middle-class children have been found to be more concerned with their school success, better integrated into the school, and to have higher educational and vocational aspirations than working-class children. Middle-class children had a more rigid value system. To them more things were considered "bad things to do," and they "believed more strongly that infringement of rules required punishment." The "middle-class child felt more accepted, he said more often than the working-class boy that he could discuss things with his parents, that he could confide in them, and that they share his interests." The working-class child "is emotionally left more to fend for himself." [15]

Because social order as defined in middle-class concepts generally ignores working-class concepts is not to condemn the definition. "Each perceives, thinks, forms judgments, and controls himself according to the frame of reference of the group in which he is participating." Personal controls are made possible by the very fact that people can define situations from the same standpoint as others. Their sharing of belief systems and value systems enables them "to conceive of their ever changing world as relatively stable, orderly and predictable." [16]

It is the apparent middle-class assumption that all Americans have an upward social drive. But many do not. When people have a negative self-evaluation, when they do not believe they have the capacity to meet a given goal, higher status, for example, the goal will become unattractive to them.[17] They may become apathetic or they may fit the old Jewish proverb: "A worm in a jar of horseradish thinks its life is the sweetest in all the world." Low aspiration can be a defense mechanism to reduce the pain of frustration.

The difficulty arises when the middle class judges members of the working class in terms of values or perspectives that the latter may not share or even perceive. This raises the question of the fairness of a judgment based on an assumed identity of standards of what is right and what is wrong, and of available choices. The fallacy of this assumption may not be noticed by the middle-class legislators, judges, and administrators, but the working class, and particularly those who live in the slums, are conscious of it.

Whenever people enter transactions together each does so with expectations. The more repeatedly these expectations are realized the more they are confirmed and reinforced. "In this way, people in each cultural group are continuously supporting one another's perspectives, each by responding to the others in expected ways." [18] Thus people of each class will tend to find support among others in their class so long as they are working within their class expectations. When they are confronted by the expectations of people of another class a conflict arises which, as other conflicts, may be settled by the superior power of one over the other, by denial of the fact that the difference exists, by compromise, or by adopting the expectations of the other group.

The conflict between school as a mediator of social values and the subculture of the working-class child becomes greater the lower his class status is. For how can he accept the reality of schooling which introduces him to the basic skill of reading through "goody-goody" or "good-humored" texts which belie the lives of his slum and shanty family and those of the slum and shanty youngsters with whom he plays? The middle-class ethos of his school may feed his dreams, and perhaps contribute to schizophrenia, but it does not accord with his experience.[19]

There are apparent exceptions, but these will be the children whose families, for historical and other reasons, in spite of poverty have a motivating upward mobility drive, as was the case with a large proportion of immigrant families from Southern and Eastern Europe whose first American acculturation was in the sweatshops and mines. Usually they belonged to ethnic groups that took care of them, helped them rise—the Italians and Jews by providing work and business opportunities, the Irish through political jobs.

Although the causes are not clear, it has been found that in high delinquency areas nondelinquents "actively dissociate themselves from their destructive environment and work towards leaving it entirely." [20] But the poor child of our urban-center slums and rural shanties who lacks motivation or has no social group to support his upward mobility scorns, as ignorant or hypocritical, his teachers and books which tell of values and relationships he has not experienced, whose goals or institutionalized means of achieving those goals, or both, he rejects. The school represents to him an alien culture. To his middle-class teacher, generally, he is part of an alien subculture, if not of an alien culture.[21] Conant advises us that "*a teacher must know something about the processes by which social behavior emerges in groups of children*." [22] * But few do, except perhaps on a cognitive level, for such knowledge if accepted would be threatening. Teachers are an upwardly mobile population and it is unsettling to have to accept without retaliation the challege these children address to middle-class values.

The textbooks used in schools may not only alienate children of slum culture or those who are nonwhites; they may also distort the values of middle-class children and their perception of social transactions. A typical textbook used in elementary schools on the subject of *neighbors* describes a white suburban middle-class family, well dressed, well housed, with proper pets and a shiny car, and their white middle-class neighbors. There is no mention of Negroes, Puerto Ricans,

* Conant's recipe for teachers might well be applicable to the training of criminal court judges, who should also "know something about the processes by which social behavior emerges."

Indians, or Mexicans as neighbors and no reference to neighboring nations. In effect the nonwhite, even the white, children who live in poverty, are declassed; and the white middle-class children are deprived of learning about neighbors who are different. A source of value conflicts, therefore, is the school that nurtures a sense of deviance in one part of society and raises the other to ignorance of differences, and, in time, to value difference as the equivalent of deviance.*

All perception has been described as hypothetical and as such subject to constant testing.[23] In school this testing process by the slum child may appear to the teachers to be stupidity or smart-aleckness which the teacher treats punitively or nonsupportively. This gives him a taste of being an outcast from that middle-class society of which the teacher is an image, and who is often his only close contact with a middle-class person. An example may be the difference in a child's and his teacher's perception of the family. A teacher was asking the class in a slum neighborhood to write the names of their parents and other family data. One little boy failed to give his father's name. Several times he was asked to do so and each time "refused." The teacher scolded him for his disobedience and sent him to the principal. The principal punished him and sent for his mother. As the mother was working the grandmother came. She too was scolded by the principal. It appeared that the boy did not know who his father was, for there had not in his lifetime been any one man in the family. The teacher and principal expected him to have a father, but reality to him was that he had none.

For a child it is only a step from testing the reality of his perceptions to testing the teacher's endurance and finally

* In some schools new textbooks are being introduced with some pictures and mention of nonwhites.

being tagged "a discipline problem." The teacher then becomes a stereotype of a reference group which does not accept but rejects the working-class child, and he in turn does not accept it and rejects its values, which to a large extent are not real to him, and are not his anyway. This tends to alienate the slum child from the prevailing social values and the community's acceptable choices. Little formal education is required for these children to win social acceptance, even prestige, among their slum associates. They have little need then for the motivation to find middle-class acceptance which is pushed on them by the schools on the assumption that it is something everyone needs and wants. Thus the school, society's instrument through which it intends young people to learn its standards, tends to fail to serve as a reference of norms for the working-class child.[24]

A Negro teacher in a Harlem school has pointed out that the middle-class views emotionalism with "repulsion." Consequently, Negro and Puerto Rican children who show strong emotions, such as anger or excitement or, as the Germans say, are *ausgeniessen*, may be regarded as abnormal, emotionally disturbed. If they fight they may be severely punished. But in the slums children have always had to learn to fight for survival.[25] Thus their norms of behavior conflict with those established by the standard setters of proper conduct.

On the other hand lack of what we conceive to be normal emotionalism may be hard for the middle-class adult to cope with and impossible to accept. The nihilism of many teenagers and young adults today consciously denies historic values and the goals of an industrial society. They experience in the culture bureaucratic, semi-automated instrumentalities of applied science and dehumanized transactions which appear to mock the expressed goals of traditional religion and democracy.

Why study, why work, why become involved, they ask. They see no choices or block them out from perception.[26]

This is not to suggest that the dominant elements of society should or could accept those subcultural standards or ignore serious violations of social norms. However, those standards are relevant to perceived choice necessary to *mens rea*, to intentional violations of social norms. For from their own viewpoint such deviants may be innocent of wrongdoing. They may be acting in accordance with the norms of their culture.

At the lowest level of slum life the child also learns early the contradictions between middle-class law and his own. The schools "even had books telling us what great guys the cops are." [27] Great guys, when someone in the family or in the house or surely on the block has been manhandled or arrested or humiliated by the police, who thus started a living (not bookish) contact with law! The people in the world of these children do not see the law as giving the poor man equality with the rich. Great guys, when the police say "open up" and walk into homes or search people and you have to do what they say! There is no choice for them between obeying the police and invoking the constitutional guaranty against search and seizure without a warrant. The law does not seem to them to be a friend of the very poor. Its values are not theirs.

Furthermore, the individual, who is without personal power or the support of some power group, who has some complaint against an agent or agency of government, is at a disadvantage. His voice is unnoticed by bureaucracy, for "voices without power have seldom ever received an attentive audience." Yet these are the people whose lives are most frequently dependent on administrative decisions affecting welfare allowances, health services, schools, police, and employment.[28] They are also more frequently involved with the lower courts. They have not sufficient knowledge or power or funds to challenge adverse rulings or arbitrary treatment through avenues of appeal available to people of higher status or with more powerful friends or who belong to influential organizations. Though the cultural goal may be acceptable and they may want to participate in it, the institutional means to participate may be unavailable. In such a situation the behavior of bureaucrats becomes an unacceptable norm of society. The price of rejection is apathy toward middle-class values and motivations, or humiliation and a sense of loss of social power ("You can't fight city hall") with resultant hostility. Legalized choices—even when created by the middle class for the benefit of the people of the slums—are not seen as choices. Goals and means merge as impossible—or, if this seems too definite, as improbable and, therefore, of little value in the culture of the poor.

Different Value Systems

The different levels of economic groups, which to some extent correspond with educational levels, have different value systems. Hyman indicates a correlation between the kind of position held by the father and the job and educational aspirations of the children.[29] William Foote Whyte and Kinsey have shown differences in sexual mores among economic or educational levels.[30]

Chein[31] has found high positive correlations between a number of socioeconomic variables and chronically deviant ("contranormative," as he calls them) patterns of youth behavior. He used four measures of deviant behavior: incidences of delinquency, school dropouts, out-of-wedlock childbirths by girls under twenty-one, and syphilis among youth. One of the variables to which these deviant behaviors related was disrupted family life. The family, of course, is the basic institution that transmits social norms, and when it it disrupted its capacity to perform this function is lessened. Another variable was the prevalence of socioeconomic squalor, a slum culture. This too has less potency to promote "the societal normative system" than a middle-class neighborhood, which rewards compliance. A third variable was "high socio-economic contrast," for people growing up in such an area are faced with competing, contradictory norms. This may make it impossible for them to accept or absorb in their personalities any of those norms, and lead to a condition of *anomie*, a condition of "normlessness or normative impotence."

These findings illustrate again that subcultures may differ in their norms and that many members of some subcultures do not choose or even recognize that normative choices are available to them; or they may reject all normative systems.

The value system of people in the slum class reduces the "*voluntary* actions which," through upward mobility, "would ameliorate" their low position, and "within the bounds of the freedom available to individuals, this value system would create a *self-imposed* barrier to an improved position." [32]

Is it realistic and is it just to judge a man's intent with the measuring rod of norms he does not have? Is it realistic and is it just to attribute to him a choice which, though it may be available, is not apparent to him? When we do so, are we not attributing to others our own views, projecting our values on to them, and then condemning them for not living by those values? [33]

Where poverty is great, motivations common to others may not affect the poor, for the rewards offered by the prevailing values or norms are not available to them. They may find in vice and other forms of deviance more satisfying values. From this they may derive a "kick" and by the same token kick at society which would not notice them otherwise, is scarcely aware of their survival or demise.

> Sometimes the life of a man is poor to such a degree that he is involuntarily obliged to put a high value on some vice, and live thereby; indeed we may say straight out that very often people become vicious from sheer ennui.[34]

It is an important legal norm that people shall respect the property of others. But has this norm the same value for those at the lower economic levels as for the middle class? How is one to teach respect for property to a child whose family has almost nothing, who shares his bed and clothes with others, whose few possessions may be thrown on the street in any weather, finally to be carted away by the authorities if his parents cannot pay their rent or find another place in which to live? Of course he may be rescued by some governmental agency which pays his rent. But a value system in which such assistance is acceptable differs from the middle-class value system and is humiliating to those who would incorporate the middle-class system as their own. Such a person's idea of property, home, planning for the future, status, privacy, self-respect based on his experience will necessarily tend to differ from those of his teachers and those who make and enforce law. "How can a worker be motivated to work to furnish or improve his home, when he cannot get an apartment or even a bed to sleep in?"[35] Or when he must share all these with others or become a public aid dependent? He or she may want a television set, a car, a refrigerator, or a dress in the current style; but will his or her attitude toward property and property owners be the same as that of the middle class?

Does a slum child, then, have the same choice as the middle-class child? Is his intention the same, or seen to be the same, as that of the middle-class child when he steals or commits malicious mischief?

Note that differences in choice are probably unrelated to intelligence. They derive from different experiences and therefore expectations, which serve to reinforce one another and to result in different perceptions. These cycles create their own barriers to such a common appreciation of terms as is necessary for effective communication. What in one culture or subculture will be accepted as normal behavior may not be seen as an alternative mode of behavior in another. However, unless insanity can be proven, does not the law ignore the fact that he whose behavior is subject to scrutiny may be unaware that there are alternatives or choices?

Take Herman Melville's story of Billy Budd,[36] condemned to die for murder though his very accuser, Captain Vere, said of his crime and him, "Struck dead by an angel of God! Yet the angel must hang!" Billy Budd was a stupid man without education, gentle, not hostile, but with no verbal capacity to reply to a cruel, unfounded accusation, unable to speak up where the "reasonable man" would defend himself. He struck out with blind strength. He had no other choice or capacity to make another choice. But a "reasonable man" might well have foreseen the consequences of his act, and so Billy Budd hung from a yardarm.*

* Though in a court of law he might have been found without intent to kill and convicted of manslaughter rather than murder, this does not contradict the analysis of the story as an example of the limits of free choice to different individuals.

Deviance

According to Becker, "deviance is *not* a quality of the act the person commits, but rather a consequence of the application by others of rules to an 'offender.' The deviant is one to whom that label has been successfully applied; deviant behavior is behavior that people so label." The deviant is condemned by those with more power or status because his very difference may be threatening, may cause them discomfort, guilt feelings, out of their own repressed impulses to murder, steal, rape, engage in homosexuality, or perform malicious mischief.[37] To the well-to-do, poverty itself may be a form of deviance.

Myrdal tells us that "In a queer contradiction of this theoretical knowledge [that the unfortunate occurrences in the lives of the poor are usually not due to inborn differences in human quality but are caused by the environment] he [the educated American] posits a sort of general moral feeling that nobody needs to be unemployed and poor unless he is a bad person." [38] This pretty well represents the common attitude toward vagrancy and drunkards.[39]

Criminal law may be conceived as "a compromise, a moving equilibrium" or a "collective conscience" of the various subcultures of a complex industrial society. For groups other than the more dominant, "intentional commission of a statutory or common law crime is not necessarily synonymous with defiance of the collective conscience." For everyone perceives the law and its observance as a function of his own needs, conscious or unconscious, dependent in considerable measure on his status and perception of himself in society,[40] on the expectations he has for himself, and on the expectations others who are in his reference group have of him. This is another aspect of his life-space. Thus, as in other areas of human perception, what law is or means to each individual is the result of a selective process determined by his experience, expectations, reference groups and image-maintaining needs. It may be difficult at times, for example, to draw a sharp line between consensual marriage and prostitution in a poverty culture.

How spontaneous reactions can be in terms of individual values, experience, and image-maintaining needs was brought home to me some years ago when I crossed the ocean on a ship with the late Mayor Frank Hague of Jersey City. He had been telling a friend of mine how industries had to pay his political party for the right to have railroad sidings at their plants. I had just returned from the Soviet Union and was describing a murder trial I had witnessed at which the defendant's friends and neighbors appeared relaxed and in fine humor. This led me to queston my interpreter as to how they could treat a murder trial so lightly. Wasn't there a death penalty? Not for this crime, I was told. It was only a case of killing in passion a girl who lived in a house on the same court. But, I asked, don't you have the death penalty? We only have the death penalty here, my interpreter said, for counterrevolution, highwaymen, and bribery. At the mention of bribery, Hague exclaimed: "My God, how barbaric!"

Not only do "high-status people have a greater stake in conformity than low-status people"; they are better able to protect themselves from conviction for crime that would label them nonconformist. They can afford attorneys who are abler or have greater prestige than those who represent low-status people. Their own prestige has greater value with judge and jury.

The following is an example of unequal application of law

which causes poor people to reject the relevance of its norms.

In the summer of 1963 a group of wealthy young people attending an extravagant house party in Southampton, Long Island, destroyed much of the furniture and interior of the house in which they were lodged. Fourteen of them were indicted. By February 1964 eleven of them still under indictment had not been brought to trial. It was hoped that they could be tried during their Easter vacation "so as not to interrupt defendants' college studies." A slum child might well wonder whether he would be treated with the same patient consideration by the law-enforcing authorities.

The police differentiate among social classes. Toch writes, "The fact that police work entails disproportionately many contacts with socially underprivileged and emotionally disturbed persons who do not display typical middle-class conduct, can shape police perception of human nature and of appropriate social behavior . . . Wesley points out that the 'police believe that certain groups of persons will respond only to fear and rough treatment. In the city studied, they defined both Negroes and slum dwellers in this category.' By thus unfavorably categorizing one segment of the community, the police create a double standard in human relations. Placement in the outgroup deprives a person of his right to customary courtesies, to friendly consideration and to frank communication." [41]

The inequality of legal representation because of poverty is widespread; yet courts have been slow to recognize the injustice of this. It was not until 1963 that the United States Supreme Court overruled not only state courts, but its own earlier decision, and held that the right to counsel in all criminal, not only capital, cases was a basic constitutional guaranty.[42]

People of higher status are less likely to be convicted for

"white-collar crimes" than are persons of low status tried for "blue-collar crimes." Income tax evasion and violation of anti-trust laws, for example, are not regarded with the same hostility as crimes of violence or petty theft. The differential in law enforcement against white-collar crimes must stir up cynicism, even if one does not consider this differential in itself cynical. It is the person bribed, not the briber, who is usually punished. Embezzlements have frequently not been prosecuted to enable surety companies to use prosecution as a threat to obtain restitution and salvage.[43] A few years ago it was the performers in a television program who were prosecuted, not the sponsoring company or producers who benefited by or who were also parties to the fraud on the public.

Divorce and alimony are open to middle-class families that can afford lawyers; desertion and orders for support are the procedures used by the poor.

> The point is, of course, extra-legal means of self-help can and must be resorted to in order for the poor to enjoy that measure of self-determination the law accords to the well-to-do.[44]

Few people regard divorce (as distinguished from the cause or method of obtaining it) as wrongful; but desertion—the poor man's divorce—is not sanctioned by law or morally approved.

The law affects the poor differently than middle-class persons in that the former "are frequently in market situations where illegal practices prevail." Consumer frauds relating to misrepresentations in prices, quality, etc. are frequent with respect to low-income consumers. They suffer from slum landlords who fail to fulfill obligations to provide services and repairs and merchants who refuse to honor warranties. They rarely challenge through legal action insurance settlements and cancellations. They have little means to have housing codes enforced. They do not get equal police protection. Under the common law the tenant must pay rent even though the landlord fails to perform his obligations, and unless there are statutes to the contrary the tenant cannot use the withholding of rent to compel compliance by the landlord with the health and safety codes. He cannot benefit by the legal fiction of constructive eviction because there may be no place to which he can go without moving into similar defective housing.[45]

Where small claims courts have been established theoretically to help the small man get a hearing without necessity of counsel, these courts are frequently used by collection agencies against the poor man. As in these and other courts of lower jurisdiction, the calendars are crowded and very little time is given to any case. This is true in the lower criminal as well as the lower civil courts. There is in them "a tendency toward mass processing of cases." Other legal agencies also dispense justice on a mass-production scale, allowing little opportunity for thorough findings of fact and law.[46]

Situational Nature of Crime

A man or woman who might be unable to imagine (i.e., whose self-image might reject) stealing a car to take a ride, breaking open a telephone coin box, or robbing a ticket seller or telephone office at gunpoint might nevertheless fail to hand his railroad ticket to the conductor at the end of a ride if through oversight it had not been collected ("If the conductor didn't ask for it, why should I give it?"); buy a half-fare ticket for a child who is old enough to require a full fare ("He doesn't look old enough for a full fare"); or keep the coins which through mechanical error had dropped in a telephone return coin box ("It was the machine's fault—they overcharge for telephone calls anyway").

Regardless of whether such acts are forbidden by law, they are ethically intentional thefts, conscious choices to take or keep something to which another is entitled. Similarly, the traveler who would think it wrong for a hotel to falsify a bill may accept his or her falsification of an import declaration as proper game against the government customs officers.[47] These are hostile acts against impersonal institutions, and in the value systems of many people are crimes of lesser severity than theft from an individual. The sense of guilt can with facility be assuaged by rationalizing the feeling that it is different to cheat an institution than a person.

In some cases the use of impersonal institutions such as corporations as instruments through which to commit crimes appears to reduce their apparent gravity. These are middle-class crimes. Thus, penalties are rarely imposed on the chief officers of corporations violating antitrust laws, and are minimal when they are imposed.

In a recent case, a group of leading manufacturers of electrical equipment were found to have acted in restraint of trade.* They had mulcted the public utilities of many millions of dollars. The corporations concerned were fined a total of $1,787,000, but only seven of the individual corporate officers responsible received prison sentences of some thirty days; others received suspended sentences; and individual fines (paid by the corporation, not the persons convicted) amounted to $137,500. None of the convicted (they would almost cer-

* Restraint of trade under the Sherman Anti-Trust Law, U.S.C.A. Title 15, Sections 1 and 2, is a misdemeanor. Intention, that is, *mens rea,* is an element of the crime. Those who engage in illegal price fixing are held to have intended the necessary and direct consequences of their acts.[48]

tainly be called "criminals" if their offenses had not been "white-collar" crimes) was a top policy maker of his corporation.[49] One may reasonably conclude that white collars are handled with kid gloves.

Another example is to be found in violations of gambling laws by churches conducting bingo games. Even where illegal, those responsible are rarely prosecuted, for their intentions are considered "good," although an individual bookmaker down the street who was trying to make a personal living would be brought to trial. The interposition of the impersonal organization serves to depersonalize the crime.

Thus we appear to be immersed in the relativity of values and the situational nature of evil intent, *mens rea.*

Symbols and Ritual Behavior

People in power tend to be conservators, to protect their power and status—particularly that form of prestige which presents to them and others an image of power. They devise symbols, prescribe manners, and create masks to avoid making true feeling explicit, fearful of the consequences if they were to reveal fear or hostility.[50] Obversely, they impose these symbols, manners, and masks on others; and through their prestige make them part of the culture, so as to avoid expressions of fear and hostility against those in power which in turn might release the latter's repressed violence and guilt.[51]

Formal etiquette may be thought of as a means of handling relations with people with whom one does not seek intimacy. It is particularly useful when adults and young, men and women, upper classes and lower classes, are sharply separated and when a code is necessary to mediate exchanges across these lines. Thus etiquette can be at the same time a means of approaching people and of staying clear of them.[52]

Such supression of feeling must distort perception and values, by emphasizing the ritual importance of symbols, etiquette, manners, and masks over the realities of feeling. Ritual behavior tends to become the cultural norm for judging behavior. If the prevailing code of manners requires a Negro to step off the sidewalk into the street to enable a group of white people to pass in order not to bring about physical contact which might result in argument or violence, then failure to observe this code is a deviance from expected behavior and may result in a charge of "disorderly conduct."

Lorenz found in fish, fowl, and some animals a pattern of redirected activity by which hostility toward a mate is redirected toward a neighbor. This avoids destructive violence between mates. It also results in a ritualized greeting or triumph ceremony which creates a bond between them.[53] This is comparable to the redirection of intrafamily or class hostility toward another class or institution. Such redirected hostility develops a bond among middle-class people who direct their hostility against the nonconforming slum population and its norms, and among the slum population against the middle class and their norms. Law is in some respects a symbolization of this redirected hostility. When people refuse to accept the symbolic expression of hostility represented by law and other governmental institutions this may become a threat to the stability of middle-class social structure. Such a threat reinforces hostility which the symbolism of law and governmental institutions was supposed to suppress, crush, or screen.

Status

A major effect of ritual behavior among status groups (here, socioeconomic classes) is that it acts as a barrier to communication. Even if every word did not have a different meaning each time it was used,[54] status is in itself such a critical experience as to result in varying expectations and perceptions of attempted communication across status lines.

When someone of high prestige fails to meet expectations it may be regarded as "bad luck," whereas when someone of low status succeeds beyond expectations he may be called "lucky." He may even be kept in his place by being given to understand, not necessarily verbally, that his "good performance was abnormal for him." [55] Status needs are met not only by attempts at upward mobility but also by maintaining status lines, by keeping others on the other side of the tracks which separate people from shared experience and satisfactions.

In spite of their greater life-space, education, and mobility, high-status people, protected behind their ritual barricades, may be less accurate in their perceptions than those of low status in awareness of each other's attitudes. This is indicated in a study by Matthews and Prothro[56] * concerning awareness of whites and Negroes in Southern states of each other's attitudes toward segregation and integration. The whites, as we know, have the high-status positions there, and great pressure is put on the Negroes to accept the values of the dominant whites. The researchers found that

> regardless of the overwhelming preference of Negroes for integration and of whites for strict segregation, neither group can cor-

* This study was made before the nonviolent action campaign of integrationists got into full swing and respective attitudes were publicized and dramatized by demonstrations, police action, and legal proceedings.

> rectly estimate the views of the other. Although both races are misinformed, the estimates of whites are much more inaccurate than those of Negroes. Only 22 per cent of the whites recognize that most Negroes favor integration, but 47 per cent of the Negroes recognize that most whites favor segregation. . . . Such grossly inaccurate estimates occur among whites at twice the rate that they do among Negroes. The greater frequency of "don't know" responses among whites than among Negroes is a more direct expression of the relative lack of information among whites.[57]

For our own purposes in considering whose free will based on whose perceived available choices determines intention, the most important conclusion is: "Just as the pattern of communication in the South leaves the superordinate group as a whole less informed about the other race's aspirations, *so does it permit them greater freedom to project their own views to others.*" [58] Such ignorance may result from a denial by the whites of facts which, because they contradict their accepted norms of behavior, would be hurtful. Recognition of a conflicting reality would force them to acknowledge a threatening dissonance not only in their own cognition but also in their social behavior.

Not only may the perception of what is wrongful be related to status and power but so too may the choices which are perceived to be available.

As has been noted, it is not the "unseen" members of society who legally define deviance and find guilt. When they do not conform to the codes set by higher-status people, when they fail to make the choices that those with higher status have determined to be correct, they become *seen* as deviants who intended to break the law, not as more or less socially rejected persons whose needs have been gratified and norms of conduct formed by peers who are alien to the high-status culture.*

Aberrant Behavior

There are a number of explanations why a person consciously refrains from behavior which deviates from the norms of acceptable social conduct. He may be afraid of being discovered and punished by legal sanctions. He may not have the skills to break a safe or forge a check. There are also internalized restraints which operate when an individual feels that deviant behavior would threaten his self-respect and his acceptance by someone or some group or subculture of society that to him is a model for his behavior. Thus a sense of guilt or shame may prevent his violation of the cultural norm or "collective conscience." [60]

Merton[61] suggests consideration of two elements of social and cultural structure relating to deviance.†

> The first consists of culturally defined goals, purposes and interests, held out as legitimate objectives for all or for diversely located members of the society. . . . They are the things "worth striving for." . . .
>
> A second element of the cultural structure defines, regulates and controls the acceptable modes of reaching out for these goals. . . . In all instances, the choice of expedients for striving toward cultural goals is limited by institutionalized norms. . . .

* This concept must not be generalized to include all low-status people or all who suffer from poverty. To a great extent the aspiration to upward mobility, a goal built into our culture, is accepted, and many low-status people attempt to communicate upwards. They are not considered deviants.[59]

† This concept is comparable to lawyers' distinction between substantive and adjective law.

> An effective equilibrium between these two phases of the social structure is maintained so long as satisfactions accrue to individuals conforming to both cultural constraints. . . . Otherwise . . . aberrant behavior ensues . . . [and] aberrant behavior may be regarded sociologically as a symptom of dissociation between culturally prescribed aspirations and socially structured avenues for realizing these aspirations.[62]

Merton divides individual adaptation into five types.[63] First, when cultural goals and institutionalized means are both accepted. No question of deviance arises here. Second, where cultural goals are rejected but institutionalized means are accepted. This he described as "ritualism." In this situation an individual keeps to the "safe routines" which are socially accepted although he rejects the ends to which they are means. Ritualism occurs when a situation appears threatening and incites distrust. Here there is no behavioral deviance but the price may be paid in emotional tension and loss in creative ability.

A third mode of adaptation is where cultural goals are accepted but institutionalized means are rejected. Deviant behavior is the result of this mix. For example, people will accept the cultural goal of monetary success but reject the legal means to achieve it. They then may engage in theft, bribery, or another crime. The fourth type is represented by those who neither accept the cultural goals nor the institutionalized means of society. They abandon them. These deviants are the drug addicts, the hoboes, and the like.

Finally, there is the type which Merton calls "rebellion." In this group fall people who reject both the goals and the means but move to newer goals and means. While they reject social standards they do not reject standards as such. These people, too, are deviants and in many ways more threatening than the others to the social structure. Where they are a relatively powerless group in the community, such as adolescent gangs and beatniks, although some of their actions may be serious, they are not a great threat to the community. But "when rebellion becomes endemic in a substantial part of the society, it provides a potential for revolution, which re-shapes both the normative and social structure." This is the situation of the current so-called "Negro revolution," which opens the way to innovation. The goals of monetary success and equality are accepted, but equality is given a new meaning, integrated equality. No longer is separate equality acceptable. The movement rejects the traditional American norms of racial equality ("separate but equal") and the means of achieving them through legal segregation, including de facto segregation. It seeks to establish new goals of equality (desegregation and integration of races) by new as well as established institutionalized means (political control through Black Power, in addition to nonviolent mass demonstrations, the law courts, and new legislation).

On the fringes of such "rebellion" are those who, while they may accept the cultural goals, reject the institutionalized means and capitalize on the rebellion by expressing their hostility with violence. There may also be those who, accepting the new goals of the rebellious, reject their socialized means as the Jacobins did when they succeeded the Girondists in the French Revolution, the Bolsheviks when they took over from the Mensheviks, and the advocates of Black Power and violence and other extreme groups threaten in order to capture the "Negro revolution" from the more conservative nonviolent actionists.

We should recognize that when the goal of monetary success is accepted and the legal means of achieving that success is rejected, crime may become a "normal" response to a felt inadequacy of the socially accepted means.[64] To put this another way, here is a situation in which the available choice and capacity to act upon choice is not the naïve one between "good" and "bad" or between behaving legally or evilly. The choice of what is "good" and of behavior leading legitimately to that "good" may just not be perceived as possible or even desirable. We again face this question of how free is such an individual's choice.

The fact that at one time or another each of us has a desire to do some illegal act of violence or deceit tends to make us ready to punish others, perhaps as expiation for our own "evil" desires, to reassure our own consciences, and to avoid the shame of being thought by others to condone such behavior.* *We tend to measure the acts of others not only by what we perceive to be socially accepted norms but by our own impulses; and thus our guilty desires may become their guilty deeds.*†

We may also wish to protect ourselves and our interests from such breakdown of the dominant moral code as might threaten our image of ourselves and our society. It is as though we said to ourselves, "If he gets away with murder then maybe I can, but I don't want to think of myself as a murderer; and what would happen to my family, my friends, my property, and my job if people went around getting away with murder." The same can be said of many other crimes, especially those relating to sex. Societies and even subcultures differ greatly in their attitudes toward adultery and fornica-

* Kinsey found that in that part of the male population that had entered high school but had had no education beyond high school there was the highest incidence of homosexuality and the most frequently verbalized disapproval of such activity.[65]

† According to Merton, "Through the adroit use of . . . rich vocabularies of encomium and opprobrium, the in-group readily transmutes its own virtues into others' vices."[66]

tion and therefore in their punitiveness toward violators of their code. The stern social sanctions with which our own and primitive societies have dealt with incest have involved individual repressions of great severity and resultant guilt and hostility toward offenders. The same internal conflict prompts punitive attitudes toward homosexuality in Western cultures today, although we know that Greece at the height of its civilization did not regard this as a punishable deviance.

Anthropology has demonstrated that the norms of cultures differ. For it is to be recalled that "judgments are based on experience, and experience is interpreted by each individual in terms of his enculturation." [67] Therefore, what may be *mens rea* in one culture (or even subculture) may be acceptable intent in another. For example, what to us is the crime of bigamy is to others legitimate polygamy. Though in all cultures the crime of incest is a serious one, the definition of kinship lines within which marriage is prohibited differs vastly and the system of each society offers no choice. Whether the society is patrilineal or matrilineal may determine mating systems which to us would appear contradictory. Thus, "cousins" on the mother's side of the family may call each other "brother" and "sister" on the father's side and marriage between such a "brother" and "sister" may be prohibited, while permissible, "sometimes even mandatory" on the other side of the family, though "the same degree of biological relationship" exists. "This is because two persons related in this way are by definition not considered blood relations." [68]

Another example of the effect of acculturation on perceived choices is to be found in the eating rituals of peoples. For example, if the only food available is pork chops, fish, and vegetables, then the only choice for an orthodox Jew would be fish and vegetables; and, if the day were Friday, the only choice for a Catholic (until 1966) would be fish and vegetables; and for an orthodox Jain only vegetables.

Moreover, values may change in any culture as the result of a disequilibrium brought about by the introduction of new phenomena. Thus the relations of the Comanches to their neighbors, their attitudes toward theft of horses and the seizure of prisoners for slaves, and the intratribal relations of generations were changed by their adaptation to a horse culture.[69] In India and Africa industrialization and the accompanying movement from rural villages to cities have commenced to break down the extended family system under which everyone contributed his earnings to the family and all were subject to the consent and punishments determined by the head of the family.

Parallel differences in experiences which determine differences in expectations, attitudes, and norms exist in our own culture. The rural neighbor who may live a mile away but shares his neighbor's problems is replaced by the anonymity of the city where next door tenants may be scarcely on a nodding acquaintanceship. The automobile and the increase in the facility of mobility it has introduced have emphasized conflicting attitudes between generations in the United States.

The dominant culture may have the power to enforce its values on deviants, but it cannot eliminate subcultural values and definitions of conformity and deviance. It cannot necessarily impose on subcultures choices of good and evil which are not apparent or institutional to them.

Parents and Peers

We are in the midst of a social flux which necessarily affects transactions between generations. Whether one considers what is occurring as a shift from entrepreneurial to bureaucratic values or from inner- to other-directedness, the processes of acculturation of succeeding generations are changing and value systems are being modified.[70] According to Riesman, "Children are no longer raised by people who hold up to them the standard of a family or a class." Such "training for inner-direction" no longer can give young people "a partial buffer against the indiscriminate influence of the peer group." [71] Popularity and acceptance by the peer group have become increasingly the motivation for behavior. Although parents may believe that they are still trying to inculcate "conscience," or inner-directedness, they are forgoing much of their responsibility as standard-setters and experiencing relief that the child's peers have taken over, the child's peers and the programs and advertisements of the mass media, which leave parents the peace if not the quiet to go about their own affairs. Consequently both parents and children suffer conflict within themselves from the contradictions. Are the traditional familial and inner values or the external peer values to control? The natural rejections that normally occur between parents and adolescent children are reinforced by the child's election to be governed by the peer group. And when people feel that they and their values are rejected, they in turn reject the values of those they feel are rejecting them.

What was visible and perceived in less complex societies and in the family in previous periods is now often only sensed, and increased mobility is equated by young people to freedom which, by their definition, frees them from sharing much that was formerly communicated to older generations. In such circumstances intergeneration communication falters. *Again, it is the older generations who, as lawmakers and judges, apply their standards of values to the behavior of the younger.*

The younger generation today rarely have the chance to see their fathers work, and collaboration between student and teacher is the exception today. In former times skilled artisans, professional people, and even farm laborers learned by working *with* experienced people. They saw them work and they learned through collaborative activity. Thus there is a distance now between generations often not bridged by a relationship of mutual love and respect without which values cannot be shared. The very permissiveness, informality, and tolerance between generations may operate to dissipate norms and cause disregard of manners which had been developed as appeasing rituals to avoid hostile expressions. Without shared norms and with reduced barriers to the display of hostility and without formalized channels for the redirection of hostility, one generation cannot readily accept choices which appear proper to another.

In adolescence, nonconformity is frequently approved by the peer group members, who regard themselves as rightfully in rebellion against the domination of parents; and where the peer group, as in the case of "gangs," is isolated from adults, the models or interpreters of social norms become other adolescents. Their sense of guilt or shame is related to the norms of guilt or shame of their reference group, their gang.[72] In other words, where the ego involvement is with a peer group or a family which condones deviance, rewards for conformity come from the standards of other deviants rather than from the "collective conscience" which establishes legal norms and defines the choices between acceptable and nonacceptable behavior.

Peer norms are not, of course, all-controlling. Parental models and parental attitudes remain important variables in the problem of deviance. "Thus, in one family a boy who brings home a stolen item will be forced to return it to its owner with apologies; in another he will be lectured but allowed to keep it; in some families there will be no questions asked; and in a few he may gain approval for his contribution to the family's possessions." [73] The family "largely transmits that portion of the culture accessible" to it, its subculture which may or may not accept the general norms of society and institutionalized means of achieving society's goals. "Quite apart from direct admonitions, rewards and punishments, the child is exposed to social prototypes in the witnessed daily behavior and casual conversations of parents. Not infrequently, *children detect and incorporate cultural uniformities even when these remain implicit and have not been reduced to rules.*" [74]

In a study of mental health in midtown Manhattan it was found that "successively lower parental status carries for the child progressively *larger* risk of impaired mental health during adulthood. . . . Successively lower parental SES [socioeconomic status] tends to carry for the child progressively *smaller* chances of achieving the Well state during adulthood." [75] The lower down the population is on the parental socioeconomic scale, the greater are the "symptomatic tendencies" of psychological impairment. Although the researchers found an insignificant statistical difference between schizophrenic thought processes of the top group and the lower group on their parental SES scale, a passive-dependent character structure was found to have "a prevalence of 40% in the bottom parental stratum and only 15% in the top." [76] The passive-dependent person may be dependent upon the authority of the law or on dominant persons or groups in his subculture. Whichever may be the form of his dependence must affect his values and the number and limits of his choices, as would psychological impairment too, though how and in what circumstances psychological impairment would affect choices cannot be well defined.*

The relation between status and delinquency is shown by a study by the Institute for Social Research at Michigan. It was found that delinquency in boys occurs when there is a failure of the adolescent boy to establish a positive relationship with a law-abiding, norm-conforming man, usually the father. In our culture boys most frequently say they want to be like a certain man because of the job he holds. The jobs they admire are white-collar jobs, high-paying salaried jobs which low-status fathers do not have, and, therefore, they do not live up to the model expectations of their sons. Where delinquency occurs among middle-class adolescents, a similar failure of fathers to be models has been found. But this is far less frequent than among low-status youth. Where ego involvement with such an adult fails, then the adolescent seeks ego support among nonconformists and accepts their values to avoid such conflict of values as would paralyze all capacity to choose and act. In terms of cognitive dissonance theory[78] he downgrades socially accepted norms and upgrades deviant peer norms. Psychologically he may deny the very existence of socially acceptable norms.[79] But these psychological adjustments may not satisfy

* The situational character of intent may also be related to physiological condition. It has been found, for example, that 63 percent of crimes committed by women in an English prison occurred during the tensions of the period of menstruation and premenstruation.[77]

needs for a self-image he can respect and may lead to hostility.

Allport tells us that "ego involvement, or its absence, makes a critical difference in human behavior." [80] Therefore an individual's ego involvement with a behavior model necessarily makes a difference in self-image and acceptance of social norms as expressed in law.

Values, Norms, and Reference Groups

Face-to-face groups are not the only behavior models, the sole reference groups, but an individual is more sensitive to acceptance and rejection by those with whom he comes face to face than by others.[81] All face-to-face relationships do not, of course, have equal weight either affirmatively or negatively. The emotional impact of praise and criticism varies with status relationships and role relationships, such as family, school, work, and military.[82] Role expectancy is crucial, just as expectancy is in the perception of physical objects and their relations. For how we fill the roles we expect of ourselves and that others expect of us may determine our ego satisfaction, sense of support, and sense of social power. Our roles also affect the selectivity of our perception and communication, and thus the values within which we have choices.

Moreover identification with a reference group may largely determine, among other things, an individual's "support of its activities" (observance of law), "acceptance of the group norms" (choosing behavior that conforms to the "collective conscience") and "his perception of the legitimacy of the role system" (attitude toward authority).[83] Thus where identification with the family as a reference group is blocked, children will tend to deviant behavior, sometimes called maladjusted, sometimes delinquent. Unsatisfactory relations among the adults of the family give rise to unsatisfactory relations between the adults and the child, and the child is subjected to contradictory demands and models which interfere with his ego development.[84] Can social norms have the same value for children reared in homes where adults have unsatisfactory relations and thus set up conflicting behavior models as for children reared in homes in which adult models are less in competition and more clearly defined? Will the choices of conduct be perceived by such a child to be the same as those perceived by a child with a more satisfying home life? The answer is to be found in the tendency in such children to maladjustment at home and in school.[85]

Codes of behavior tend to be observed because people have a readiness to conform. When they have no independent guidelines or measures of value, they will ordinarily accept those of the group or subculture of which they are a part, or those of some other reference group which serves as a model.[86]

Sherif, in a classic experiment, studied the relationship of the perception of people who first made observations singly and then in groups to those who first observed in groups and then singly. His conclusion was

> There is a tendency to converge toward a common norm and to experience the situation as regulated and ordered by this norm. The group must be right. "There's safety in numbers." . . . Once the common norm is established, later the separate individuals keep on perceiving it in terms of the frame of reference which was once the norm of the group.[87]

The behavior of apparent status figures will influence conformity to or violation of a standard. Thus failure by other pedestrians to obey traffic lights reading "Wait" and "Walk" was far greater when a well-dressed man apparently of high economic status ignored them than when the same man dressed in soiled, patched working clothes did.[88] "These findings lead to the conclusions that the power of a prohibition to produce conformance is influenced both by how others react to the same prohibition and by the perceived status of persons who serve as models." [89] Social pressures to conform even in the absence of specific socially declared penalties are inherent in social living. This follow-the-leader pattern would be especially apparent in people highly dependent on authority, as well as when they have upward-mobility drives.[90] Their needs for social equilibrium require them to conform, impel them "not to stick their necks out."

However, group norms and status-power influence may be less effective in controlling judgments and conformance (1) where a person not highly dependent has as the result of experience unshared by others the means to establish values apart from his group or subculture; or (2) where he has little expectation of upward mobility to the reference group. *At either extreme the common denominator of right and wrong may be ineffective as a model of conduct.* These generalizations are always subject to modification by the experience of each individual and the situation, for there will be occasions in which the conformist will deviate and the nonconformist will behave in accordance with the social norm. Their need for equilibrium, their homeostatic needs, will not drive them uniformly to reject all socially acceptable standards and judgments, for nobody, except perhaps a schizophrenic, can be immune to his perception of what others expect of him and constantly defy their expectations. Saints and sinners living among other people wear clothes of some kind no matter how ridiculous their apparel may appear to others.

Communication Barriers and Patterns

Through the instrument of law the middle class requires all members of society to accept its values. However, the communication patterns between status levels may make such acceptance unlikely even where no other factors are involved. It is not only in underdeveloped countries that the educated "elite generally have little first-hand knowledge of the culture of their own poor, for the hierarchical nature of their society inhibits communication across class lines." [91]

In an experiment conducted by Cohen,[92] the subjects performed a task under instructions supposed to emanate from a group in another room but in reality prepared by the experimenters. The other group was said to have a more interesting job and had the power to give instructions and to replace its members from among the group of subjects. Some of the subjects were told that they would be considered for the better jobs in a further experiment. These were described as the Low Mobiles. The others were told that because of the small number of vacancies that would occur they had little chance of being selected for the other group. These were called the Low Non-Mobile Group. The subjects could communicate in writing with the supposed higher status group and among themselves.

Cohen found several phenomena of interest to us here: First, "the Low Mobiles appear to be behaving in a way guaranteed to promote their chances of being rated favorably by the powerful highs and therefore being moved to the higher group." They were more "careful about criticism"; communicated more about the task and devoted less attention to their own group than the Low Non-Mobiles. The latter appeared to react to a situation in which "no matter what they do, they cannot locomote upward." Though they worked hard, much of their energy was used in irrelevant comments. They were more critical of the high-status power group and tended "to perceive the highs as more threatening and rejecting than the Low Mobiles" did.

Secondly, even the Low Mobiles were less careful about their upward communication when they perceived that their communication would be ineffective, would not satisfy their mobility needs.

Thirdly, the Low Mobiles tended to greater dependency on the high level and communicated "more desires for support" and expressed greater confusion; whereas the Low Non-Mobiles were "predisposed toward aggression and tended not to ask for support." *

> The general picture indicates that the Low Non-Mobiles tend to become even more distant from and hostile toward the other level when they are generally disturbed and when they have specific regressive defenses. This is in contrast to the Low Mobiles, who when disturbed and regressive lean even more than they ordinarily do upon those at the upper level.[94]

As in the case of so many scientific findings, these confirm and sharpen our commonsense experience. We know that people who have a chance to move up in the world tend to imitate and play up to those who have status and the power to help them in their upward moves. They tend to adapt to the norms of those who present a model of success. We know, too, that people who are trying to move upward are more likely than

* Mention has already been made of the working-class child's experience of being "emotionally left more to fend for himself." [93]

people who have no such expectations of substantial improvement of their position to depend upon and try to obtain the support of those who can forward their mobility needs. People are likely, as we also know, to be hostile toward the power they do not feel can or will help them, and especially the power that can, but will not, help.[95] We know too from our experience, that when people who have wanted to move upward have failed, they frequently not only become less careful about the manner in which they approach and refer to the people with power or higher status, but may become even more violently hostile than those who never had an expectation to rise.

We know this from our experience as well as from research. Nevertheless we expect of the Low Non-Mobiles in our society an acceptance of people with status and power, and the laws they have made. But, in the current idiom, what's in it for them, the Low Non-Mobiles?

It is all very well to believe that a man may not be an island unto himself, in Donne's phrase, but he may, sharing an island with other Low Non-Mobiles, adopt the old British newspaper headline that a heavy fog on the Channel isolates the Continent. Though the line between class norms may be a ragged one, in many areas such a line exists and is a barrier to communication. Therefore we must again conclude that people do not necessarily have the same freedom of choice between the same standards of right and wrong.

"Poverty becomes a dynamic factor which affects participation in the larger national culture and creates a subculture of its own. One can speak of the culture of the poor, for it has its own modalities and distinctive social and psychological consequences for its members." There are "remarkable similarities," for example, to be found in the subculture of the poor, including value systems, in London, Puerto Rico, Mexico City, and "among lower-class Negroes in the United States." [96]

Blau described a law-enforcement agency where an agent in doubt as to a problem, rather than go for advice to his superior and thus admit his inability to solve the problem, preferred to go to another agent who was regarded as more highly competent. The one in doubt gained the advice from his more competent colleague and paid the price of admitting his inferiority. The more competent adviser gained the acknowledgment of his competence, which gave him prestige, but paid the price of loss of time from his own work. Thus the more advice the adviser gave, the greater the cost to his own work, while "the repeated admission of his inability to solve his own problems . . . undermined the self-confidence of the worker [the advisee] and his standing in the group." [97] So the less competent agent, unwilling to continue paying this price, went less frequently for assistance. Thus communication between status levels was restricted.[98]

Similarly it would seem that to either or both sides of a communication transaction the price required to be paid to cause change of, or agreement on, values, may appear excessive. For it would require on the one hand recognition by those of higher status and power of the perceptions and values of people of lower status and little power and, on the other hand, an admission by those of lower status and power of their inferiority. Between persons of the middle class and the slums, communication is the more difficult because the very perceptions and experiences from which their values are derived result in different meanings. For example, as has already been pointed out, law and policemen who enforce it may appear to the middle class as protectors, but to people of low economic status as threatening, unjust, contradictory of values.

Even if a man does not see that there is a choice available to him, he will be deemed by the law to have had the choice if the triers of fact find that such choices would have been available to a "reasonable man." *How reasonable a man appears to be will depend upon how much overlap there is between his perceptions and those of the man or men judging him.*

Conclusions

Unhappily, then, the conclusion must be that for whatever reasons and rationalizations of the law, a man who perceives no choice, no alternate behavior, may have no choice but to be executed because he is not the right kind of "reasonable man." [99] The right kind of reasonable man may, of course, make the wrong kind of choice and be executed too; but he at least will be judged by men who share his choice-field, share his perceptions and values.

Law, it appears, operates *As If* there were a reasonable man, and a middle-class reasonable man at that, and assumes both the probability that he has freedom of choice (that is, middle-class choices) and the capacity to act with regard to his choice. Condorcet believed that by applying the mathematical theory of probability, the mathematician's *As If*, to the processes of legal judgments, errors might be minimized. To this end he proposed a great increase in the size of any tribunal in order to assure many views which would neutralize extremes and prejudices and arrive at the truth. This concept was later applied to him by a revolutionary tribunal consisting of a large number of judges, all holding the same extreme view, and he was consigned to the guillotine.[100]

The theory of probability would appear to be no more reliable than the *As If* "reasonable man" as an instrument of justice, though in Condorcet's case it did prove that many heads may be safer than one. If to act intentionally means a free choice of action—even if the only choice is between doing and refraining from doing a specific something—then it must be seen by the actor to be a choice he is capable of acting upon as well as by those who, sitting in judgment, find the act to be intentional, the outcome of an evil choice, *mens rea.*

III ◫ *Relations of the Unconscious to Intention*

THUS FAR we have been considering intention on the assumption that it involves conscious choice, however limited the choices may be. But more and more we are becoming aware of the relationship of unconscious motivation to behavior. How valid are our legal assumptions about intention and motivation, considering what we know of the unconscious?

Though we have today considerable knowledge of the unconscious and evidence of how it operates, this is by no means as much as we know about conscious processes. Most of the evidence that we have concerning the unconcious has been accumulated since the beginning of the century, and we can scarcely condemn the law for paying little attention to such recent and incomplete data. There is something to be said for the certainty of established doctrine, however psychologically erroneous, as against the uncertainty of novel hypotheses which may appear lacking in juridical certainty, may require repeated revision, and in any event necessitate a considerable change in the processes of evaluating intent. After all, it is men who make, interpret, administer, and are subject to law, who require balance in their lives, who need and strive for self-constancy.

Legal scholars and judicial councils, however, may properly be criticized for conservatism that blocks experimental testing of the validity of legal presumptions and the process of litigation. Certainly research—especially experimental research—might profitably study the role of the unconscious in motivating crime and compromising the trial process.

Cardozo, who certified to the moral character of those judges whom he knew, recognized that both external and internal facts might affect the determination of judges. "[E]very day," he wrote, "there is borne in on me a new conviction of the inescapable relation between the truth without us and the truth within." [1]

Jacques Maritain, the distinguished Catholic philosopher, stressed the interrelationship between conscious reason and the unconscious.

> Reason does not only consist of its conscious logical tools and manifestations, nor does the will consist only of its deliberate conscious determinations. . . . Thus it is that we must recognize the existence of an unconscious or preconscious which pertains to the spiritual powers of the human soul and to the inner abyss of personal freedom. . . . Thus we must be grateful to Freud and his predecessors for having obliged philosophers to acknowledge the existence of unconscious thought and unconscious psychological activity.[2]

We have noted how the law regards acts to be intentional which are not accidental, those which we call acts of God. But we all know that the Lord acts in wondrous ways, some of the most wondrous being man's capacity to forget his intentions (such as to mail a letter) or to ignore them (as when he takes that extra drink before driving) and his frequent acts of self-punishment without consciousness of intent. Criminals are constantly performing crimes in a manner to get themselves caught, and children invite punishment without realizing they are doing so.

CONTINUUM OF UNCONSCIOUS-CONSCIOUS BEHAVIOR

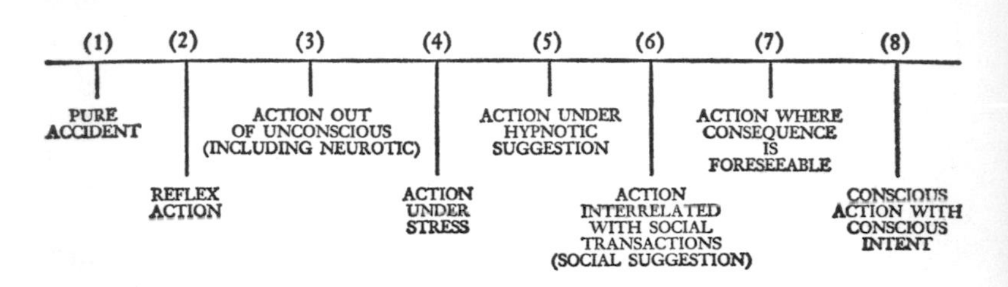

INCREASING CONSCIOUSNESS OF BEHAVIOR

We can consider happenings as a continuum extending from no intent through unconscious to conscious intent. (See diagram.) On the one extreme of the continuum will be (1) such an accidental happening as a landslide which forces a car over the precipice without the intervention of a human hand. At the other pole is (8) the premeditated act, the carefully prepared ambush or the calculated plan to defraud, the designed precipitation of the car off the road. In between are (2) reflex actions; (3) behavior motivated by the unconscious; (4) behavior under stress, such as panic and hysteria; (5) hypnosis and other forms of suggestion; (6) behavior as an adaptation to group and cultural norms or resulting from interpersonal transactions; and (7) acts with foreseeable consequences but without specific intent (presumed to be intended).

It will be noted that the first items involve little or no conscious choice and that *gradually there is an increasing degree of conscious choice possible.* (Put in another way: There is a change in the mix composed of awareness and what we take into account in our judgments and actions without awareness.)* *In any given case, the lines between these behavior categories may be blurred and they may intermingle.* The unconscious, what we are unaware of, may prompt what appears to be fully conscious choice. Except perhaps when a subject is in the deepest trance, he can refuse to perform an act suggested by the hypnotist which is contrary to his will. Even in situations in which the capacity to make a choice appears perfectly clear, it cannot be said that there are no unconscious repressions interfering with freedom of choice or action. Nor can we say with certainty that there is no choice in what appears to be reflexive action, for the extent of conscious control varies among individuals and situations. We might express this in terms of layers or blankets through which choice may be perceived by the actor but by which freedom of action is hampered. When we consider reflex actions or behavior under stress, a particular pattern may have been set by the social norms of reference groups (manners, other ritual behavior, mass flight, lynching, xenophobic excesses) or by reference to the unconscious when, as Alexander and Staub have indicated, the strength of the ego has been relaxed [4] or by suggestion ("Look out!"; "The cops are coming!"). Such a schema may be a helpful tool of analysis, in spite of this overlapping and the parallel life of the unconscious that lives "far beneath sunlit surface thronged with explicit concepts and judgments" and where are the "sources of knowledge and creativity, of love and suprasensuous desires." [5] If the action of a specific man is to be adjudged rather than that of an abstract man, an understanding of these points on the continuum may help not

* While we experience awareness, it is by no means certain what awareness is, or morphologically at what stage it begins.[3]

only to determine whether *mens rea* exists in a particular case, but also in determining the most effective treatment of the actor.

1. Pure Accident

Conscious intent is not involved in the purely accidental. We are not concerned with situations in which there is evidence of carelessness or recklessness which might justify a finding of responsibility or of fault liability except to reiterate that what appears to be purely accidental may have an unconscious purpose. Thus what appears to be purely accidental may originate in unconscious drives to punish oneself or others. The accident of the accident-prone person might never have occurred had he not been motivated by unconscious hostility.[6]

2. Reflex Action

The unconscious may also be the motivating force behind reflexive behavior. For concealed in the self-protecting act may be the unconscious intent to harm. Let us suppose that a man tripped or was jostled, and in order to keep his balance grabbed a ladder, thereby toppling it and throwing the painter on the ladder to the ground and killing him. Here is a reflexive action to protect the actor from falling. He takes hold of the nearest object to help him keep his equilibrium. He has not planned to kill the painter. The situation is not such that he might foresee that the reasonable consequence of his act would be to topple the painter. He just acted. Nevertheless, can one be certain that he was free from unconscious hostility toward some other person, which caused him to put more pressure on the ladder than was necessary to maintain balance?

Where an act is without intent or knowledge that it is reckless or dangerous, there can be no malice (at least no malice at law), and the act will be deemed automatism.[7]

3. Action Out of the Unconscious

Many actions are not accidental, reflexive, or consciously intended, but may be motivated by the unconscious. When these acts arise from the unconscious, from that area of repressed needs, there is no control of them. They are compulsive, neurotic. Under the prevailing law of the *M'Naughten Rules*, one who acts compulsively will be held responsible for his deeds. This is based on the fiction that if he knows the difference between right and wrong, he is sane; but assuming he is sane it does not follow that he is capable of making a choice or, if he perceives a choice, that he is competent to avail himself of it.

The first question to be answered in any criminal trial and in many civil actions is, "Did you do that?" After this question has been answered the question may occur, "Why did you do that?" Of course, this is not the first time that these questions arise. Parents and teachers ask these questions throughout children's formative period. The truthful answer may well be "I don't know" or "I didn't realize I was doing that." Only the conscious motives will be apparent and can be verbalized. "The unconscious motives which not infrequently exert a greater dynamic influence on our actions remain unknown. That is why it is even impossible for the offender to give a really valid, causal explanation of his acts." [8]

Human dynamics is a constant process of relieving tension by developing ego defenses, by avoidance or reinforcement, and also by devising new actions, trying new forms of behavior. This is the process by which we maintain balance among internal stresses and between internal and external stresses. Our *reinforcements* come largely from the approval of other people and from the successful repetition of actions that have released tension in the service of some need. A particular pattern of behavior may get for us what we want, and we then repeat that pattern in similar or other situations.

Avoidance is a more complicated matter. It may be through *denial* of reality, not necessarily consciously. For example, you perceive several things happening at one time. Some of them will support your attitude, will meet your expectations, and others will be contradictory. You therefore ignore the latter; you deny them, and next time you may not even perceive them.*

Another more or less conscious defense which can reduce tension in the system is *identification* with the perceptions and values of another person or a group. The child gets satisfaction and security by identifying with a parent, often with a teacher. The adult does so in merging his identity with another or others and acting as he perceives the other does or would in the situation. That, of course, is closely related to the process of adaptation to the norms of a reference group. (See pp. 61ff.)

* For a historical example, see Barbara W. Tuchman's *The Guns of August:* "The Germans were obsessively concerned about violation of international law. They succeeded in overlooking the violation created by their presence in Belgium in favor of the violation committed, as they saw it, by Belgians resisting their presence." [9]

In common terms we refer to this as "hero worship," the charismatic relation of followers to religious, political, or gang leaders, often to symbolic figures. Identification is particularly powerful in extreme situations where strong emotional pressures are involved and deviance appears threatening, as in Nazi Germany, medieval Christendom, and Southern segregationism. To identify with Hitler or the Pope or a segregationist governor reinforces. It also avoids a conscious, tension-producing conflict.

Another defense mechanism is *projection.* Instead of facing the fact of your own hostility, you project that hostility on to others. They are the hostile ones—not you. You might wish to be a law breaker, but rather than face that, you accuse the other fellow of breaking the law. Thus you project on to others your hostility which to your conscious self is unacceptable. Through this defense mechanism, "By attributing his own consciously unacceptable motives to others, the individual is able to avoid perceiving them as belonging to him." [10] This process of projection is not limited to face-to-face transactions.*

From our infancy, we indulge in a *repression* process by which threatening conflict is obliterated out of consciousness, the fearful consequences of released violence as a resolution of the conflict are buried with the conflict "far beneath sunlit surface," and rarely, except through therapy, can we recover awareness of the threatening situation which caused the repression. Of course, people vary "in their degree of tolerance of fear"; some "have strong egos and consciously contain in-

* To General Hausen, in Belgium in 1914, there could be "absolutely no doubt . . . that the whole population of Dinant and other regions was 'animated—by whose order?—by one desire to stop the advance of the Germans.' That people could be animated to stop the invader without an order from 'above' was inconceivable." [11]

tense fear for extended periods of time." [12] They do not have the same need to repress as do those with weaker tolerance. Their perception of reality is broader and more accurate. Their motivation and intent are more conscious.

Repression is one way of attaining equilibrium, a steady homeostatic state. As one may avoid threat or stress by removing oneself from a physical situation, so one may avoid threat and stress by removing awareness of the situation. According to Freudian theory, a function of the ego is to "strive to establish balance among the three 'tyrants'—id, super-ego, and outer environment. Likewise the so-called mechanisms of ego defense are essentially maintainers of a steady state. Even a neurosis has the same basic adjustive function." [13] When the ego fails in its mission and any of the three "tyrants" takes control, then the balancing function of the neurosis substitutes motivations of the unconscious for those of the conscious system.

The workings of the unconscious, whether by repression of material which might force a decision, a choice among conflicting behaviors, or by providing motivation for behavior, contribute to the maintenance of balance, the stability of the self-image. This may even be at the expense of biological survival,[14] as in war, or when one risks his life to protect the life of one he loves, or engages in a gang war to establish status in his gang, or robs a bank to build up his image of himself as a man who can defy the law. Although there is no risk to biological survival in the commission of fraud or evasion of income taxes or laws against restraint of trade, these lawless acts too may be in the service of ego-maintenance. These are also hostile acts in defiance of legal, social norms.

Whereas in general a person intending to behave in a particular manner consciously or unconsciously estimates his chance of success, one who acts for a compulsive purpose, though he may estimate his chance of success to be nil, will nevertheless do what he knows must fail his purpose. "The compulsion appears to the conscious personality as something foreign, the Ego perceives the impulse and despite that it perceives it as something foreign, it is unable to stop it from motor expression. Kleptomania, hydromania, compulsive lying, and betrayal, belong to this type of crime. . . ." [15] Theft and robbery may occur as a result of fetishism. These of course are compulsive acts and not free choice. Neurotic compulsion therefore can be deemed the seat of numerous crimes.

Freud considers delinquency as behavior originating in a paradoxical reaction between a guilty conscience and punishment.

> He [the delinquent] is not only undeterred by punishment, but is encouraged by it to break the law again. One important reason for his criminality is his need for punishment by which he tries to relieve guilt feelings for deep-seated unconscious tendencies. To be punished for a smaller crime instead of the greater one he unconsciously wants to commit, is a good bargain for him. Moreover, punishment diminishes the restrictive force of his conscience. After being severely punished, he feels even with society and is freer than before to act antisocially. It would be erroneous, however, to draw the conclusion that such persons should not be made responsible for their acts. It only indicates that the disposition of different types of criminals must be individually determined according to the nature of the offender.[16]

Can a distinction be made between the intention to do an act known to be wrong for the purpose of achieving the fruits of that act, on the one hand, and, on the other, to do a wrongful act because it will arouse retribution? Even though the purpose of the act may be in the unconscious, the act has a purpose. It is no more fortuitous than a consciously intended act. The purpose may be self-punishment rather than personal gain or injury to another, but the consequence to the other person will be the same. Can one distinguish between an act arising out of an unconscious compulsion, a conscious drive to injure somebody, and a conscious intent to do so for some other purpose, a good purpose, perhaps, such as euthanasia? The compulsive act may appear to be fortuitous, but it is no more so in a psychological sense than an act of willful intent, the premeditation of law.

Accidents themselves are not always accidental. Thus there is a higher incidence of automobile accidents involving drivers with hostile personalities.[17] It is suggested that accident-prone people, people who tend to become involved in accidents seemingly avoidable, are responding to "a need to expunge unconscious feelings of guilt." Often these accidents occur in situations familiar to them. Often, too, unconscious guilt may cause people to take unreasonable risks.[18] How can there be the free choice implicit in intent if the unconscious blots out the consequences of such hazardous behavior reasonably to be anticipated?

It would appear therefore that the line between intent and the fortuitous may be indeterminable and the attempt to describe or declare it unrealistic. It may be a fiction arising from a need to establish fault and an inability to discover the truth of a specific person's motivation. Are we not reminded of the pattern of primitive societies which treated the accidental, happenings for which there was no patent explanation, as acts of the spirit world working through man? We too forgive the spirit world of the unconscious if our rituals of law and trial cannot uncover a causal relationship between the accused and the act. The unconscious, of course, gives clues to its motives, and from these triers of fact can and do make inferences of intent. But inferences can be good or bad guesses and may themselves be prompted by the unconscious motives of judge or jurymen.

An example of what we know now to be a nonaccidental accident is the slip of the tongue, "when the impulse coming from the unconscious part of the personality catches the Ego unawares and breaks through to action." So, too, with some crimes.

> When we compare an accidental crime, i.e., a slip which results in a criminal act (manslaughter) with other crimes, we shall find that the characteristic thing about the former is that the Ego in such cases does not participate actively. . . . The Ego, in such cases, is merely overcome by heretofore repressed tendencies; this happens at a special moment, which is characteristic for this psychological accident. We shall recall that when the Ego finds itself suddenly weak (over-fatigue, distractibility), when it is preoccupied with a specially difficult task and is thus concentrated on one special point, then many slips of the tongue and action occur. . . .[19]

The unconscious is a world of separate symbolism[20] removed from reality, uncontrollable by the cognitive processes, that is, by reason, by the conscious, but able to replace the conscious and irresistibly to induce behavior. The unconscious is untouchable because it is created as an escape, a method of avoidance, as a haven from reality, and thus divorced from contact with reality. Its choices are those of dreams, or it is a depth frozen without choices. Even when the conscious perceives possible choice, the unconscious may have a veto power over action. What a man purposes when in the clutches of his unconscious gives him no more freedom of choice of action than if he were disarmed before another man with a loaded gun. An example of this is Dostoevsky's grim story *Notes from the Underground*.[21]

For such a man his crime is compulsive behavior, a symptom of his neurosis. "The characteristic thing about the *neurotic criminal* is that he identifies himself only partly with the criminal act he commits." [22] But still we administer law with the fiction that the compulsive neurotic, who may be able to distinguish consciously right from wrong, is capable of behaving according to socially acceptable norms if he but wills to do so, if he has the intent to observe the law.

This prevailing view in Anglo-American law ignores the essential difference between normal and neurotic behavior. Essentially a normal person has flexibility in contrast with the neurotic whose behavior is frozen "into patterns of inalterability which characterizes every manifestation of the neurotic processes. . . . No moment of behavior can be looked upon as neurotic unless the processes that have set it in motion also predetermine its automatic repetition, irrespective of the situation, the utility, or the consequences of the act." [23]

Behavior may be impelled by the unconscious, but there need not be consciousness of behavior so impelled. The latter may in some respects be similar to reflexive action. An example of the former, as given by Kubie, is the case of "a soldier who is in training camp who is pathologically afraid of his sergeant" and "shoots himself in the foot. The act is deliberate but the fright and the lack of control are not. These are products of deep neurotic problems." Another pertinent example of the effects of the unconscious relates to Charles Darwin, whose unconscious obliterated arguments opposing his theories and who had to write them down to recall and consider them.[24]

What the neurotic may be able to see but frequently cannot evaluate effectively is the "reasonable" consequences of his behavior, that is consequences which might normally be expected to issue from his behavior. The legal fictions concerning the consequences which a reasonable man should foresee will be discussed later. What is now suggested is that one who is prompted to action or inaction by his unconscious may be unable to relate his unconscious drives to the reality expectations of that conduct. An example would be high school youngsters who, subject to unconscious drives, seek release from sexual tension without the realistic estimate of the chance that nine months later the girl will bear a child, or that the boy may be prosecuted for second-degree rape.

Reference has already been made to the distorting effect of the unconscious on perception. The paranoiac, for example, may see motivation in the accidental.

> It is a striking and generally recognized feature in the behavior of paranoiacs, that they attach the greatest significance to trivial details in the behavior of others. Details which are usually overlooked by others they interpret and utilize as the basis of far-reaching consequences.[25]

The defensive mechanism of repression, therefore, distorts perception and deprives behavior of an intentional quality. *Freedom of choice is not present when action is dictated principally by unconscious drives. The very powers of judgment, of problem solving, which are inherent in formulating an intent, are absent.*

4. Action Under Stress

Under conditions of severe stress reason may abdicate and customary norms of behavior be overcome, blanketed. The ego may lose control.[26]

As stress increases, our perceptions of a situation become less accurate,[27] and we may not perceive the cues to those norms and values which customarily guide us. Murphy discusses experiments with animals and human beings who

> when frustrated after making wrong responses, were sometimes in such distress that the need to escape mounted, the inner factors being reinforced and the outer cues serving no purpose—they went on furiously doing the wrong thing time and again. The sheer stress of a situation may prevent the ordinary lability to which the term "trial-and-error" learning is applied. The child or adult may fixate, because of sufferings, the very response that causes the suffering.[28] *

A relevant phenomenon is Merton's self-fulfilling prophecy "whereby fears are translated into reality" [30] and in which there is "a *false* definition of the situation evoking a new behavior which makes the originally false conception come *true*. The specious validity of the self-fulfilling prophecy perpetuates a reign of error." [31] This is another aspect of conduct fulfilling expectations. Can it be said that such a process necessarily involves free choice or conscious intent?

We might put this in another way: *In conditions of severe stress, we not only do not perceive phenomena as we normally do and, consequently, are unable to react effectively in a situation. Our very valuations may, during the period of stress, so determine or distort our perceptions that our rational proc-*

* An experiment with rats that were frustrated by being compelled to attempt solution of an insoluble problem is disheartening, for one could substitute the behavior of humans and find similar fixations. Even when the reward was made accessible without any barriers and the problem became soluble "the stereotyped habit [had become] inflexible and maladaptive to changes in the situation. . . ." "Here on the rat level," the experimenters say, "we seem to have rigidly stereotyped behavior, experimentally induced through prolonged frustration, that looks remarkably like the compulsory fixed habits, ineradicable through usual means, that are often observed in human beings." [29]

esses become ineffective—if not inoperative—and we lose our capacity to choose.

We see this in conditions of panic and hysteria in which riot may occur or persons may use more force than is necessary to subdue an assault. The Oxford Dictionary defines panic:

A sudden or excessive feeling of alarm or fear, usually affecting a body of persons, originating in some real or supposed danger vaguely apprehended, and leading to extravagant or injudicious efforts to secure safety.[32]

Webster's New World Dictionary gives a slightly different definition:

A sudden, unreasoning, hysterical fear, often spreading quickly.[33]

Though it has been questioned whether "panic" applies to individuals,[34] in common parlance we speak of an individual having "panicked." We mean that he has acted in a compulsive manner out of "hysterical fear" and, except for the absence of "a body of persons" the same elements are present as in panic behavior by a "body of persons." The elements of panic include first of all "fear." It is an "excessive" or "unreasoning" fear. It is "excessive," that is, inappropriate to a reasoned, balanced reaction to the situation. "If the intensity of the fear behavior is in harmony or fits the environment, it is not excessive; if it is more than is required by the environment, it is excessive." [35] This would be so where a man shoots an ordinary trespasser to drive him off of his land or, having struck in self-defense, hammers the offender to death.

Panic fear leads to this "extravagant or injudicious" action for the purpose of securing "safety" from the cause or supposed cause of the fear. It spreads "quickly," thus "usually affecting" others. Whether we would describe an individual as being in panic or as being in hysteria, he is unable behaviorally or cognitively to engage in trial-and-error methods to discover the appropriate risk or judicious behavior for the occasion. He is so "fixated" on securing safety that he sees no choices and may continue "furiously doing the wrong thing time and again." Jordan said:

> The terror and frenzy evoked by the fear situation lead to safety-seeking actions over which the actor loses all personal control. We have here an important tie-in with rationality in behavior. Rational behavior implies that a person has a choice over his actions and then chooses one of many possible actions on the basis of "rational" criteria. To the extent that a person has no choice over his actions he therefore cannot behave rationally. In a situation where a person has no control over his actions, where he is forced to do whatever he is doing, there is no place for rationality.[36]

In other words, panic and hysteria* present situations in which there is little or no freedom of choice. Strong emotions of fear, a strong need to escape, a powerful fixation, an "emotional excitability, excessive anxiety" leave no room for free will, for cognitive control over the operation of an evil hand. For under severe stress reality may not be perceived, or what is perceived may be suppressed and denied.

Wolberg made a study of various people under hypnosis.

* "hysteria. 1. a psychiatric condition variously characterized by emotional excitability, excessive anxiety, sensory and motor disturbances, and the simulation of organic disorders, such as blindness, deafness, etc. 2. any outbreak of wild, uncontrolled excitement or feeling, such as fits of laughing and crying; hysterics." *Webster's New World Dictionary of the American Language.*

A psychological definition of hysteria is: "Nervous and mental disorder with a variety of symptoms: dissociation, suggestibility, somnambulisms, anesthesias, paralyses; when there is a loss of functions (as in anesthesia or paralysis) the psychoanalysts refer to conversion hysteria (repressed processes converted into symptoms)." [37]

He gave them contradictory instructions—that they would have a strong desire to eat a cake of chocolate next to them and also that they would not want to take the chocolate because it would be wrong to do as it did not belong to them. This created a severe conflict and resultant anxiety. One subject, when he came out of hypnosis, gave no apparent attention to the chocolate either in behavior or conversation. When Wolberg asked him whether he didn't want the chocolate he replied, "What chocolate?" The chocolate that was next to him was pointed out and he responded, "I don't see any chocolate." When the chocolate then was dropped on the floor by Wolberg, the man exclaimed that he had heard something land but he didn't see it.

Why had he developed this reaction? To avoid conflict. Hysterics quite characteristically respond to conflict by acting as if factors which stimulate it do not exist, often by deadening their senses. The hysterical symptom, like not feeling, not seeing, not hearing, not smelling, is a defense against perceptions whose acknowledgment would touch off anxiety. By temporarily not seeing the chocolate, this man avoided trouble, at the expense of his total functioning.[38]

Resistance to the police and flight are often examples of panic and hysteria built into the processes of law enforcement. In such cases the punitive approach of the law—the purpose of which is to deter crime by arousing a sense of fear of punishment or guilt—achieves its purpose of inspiring fear. In such a situation the law's punitiveness may not have been sufficient to restrain the criminal act, but it is effective in stimulating a need to avoid the penalty. When we feel guilt we feel the fear of retributive action by our parents or some other authority figure. We never outgrow the impulse to avoid a threatening situation by separating ourselves from it[39] by flight, as from the police, or desertion of the family, or by attempting to kill or otherwise destroy or change the person or thing or situation which is threatening.

5. Action Under Hypnotic Suggestion, Brainwashing, etc.

Hypnosis is not a state of sleep. It is more of a preconscious state with this difference—that in the hypnoidal state the subject is more than normally sensitive to suggestion and his attention is concentrated to respond to cues given by the hypnotist. His mind may be functioning, he may be aware of the people and happenings around him. "Commands and dictates of the hypnotist, unless they be distasteful to the subject, are generally accepted and acted upon less critically than in waking life." [40] In satisfaction of his unconscious needs the subject may wish to establish and maintain a relationship of dependence on the hypnotist. He lacks a desire to take initiative and to plan. There is a tendency toward inertia. He can gratify unconscious wishes and shift the blame to the hypnotist. "The patient seems to invest the hypnotist with benevolent protective powers and to relate to the hypnotist, to some extent, at least, with expectant trust. People seem to have a need for this kind of relationship as a residue of their childish desire to be loved and protected." [41]

Not all people are subject to hypnosis. Some are more responsive than others. It has been estimated that "well over one-half of the population is capable of experiencing a trance of some degree which tends to deter, for at least a while, their usual capacity for critical judgment." [42] The degree of hypnotic effect can range from total awareness and responsibility for an action to limited awareness and questionable responsibility. People who are subject to a deep trance are highly tractable and their responses are uncritical to signals and demands even when they might be against their best interests. "It is as if a temporary suspension of his normal sense of protection has occurred. In fact, the subject abandons all of his control over himself to the hypnotist." [43]

Bryan says that while the patient is motivated to accept suggestions by the hypnotist, such motivation "does not exist in hypnosis for criminal activity unless, of course, an underlying criminal tendency exists." Spiegel, on the other hand, appears to believe that a person who can be subject to a deep trance may in that state be induced to act against his interest because his "sense of awareness is severely limited," he is uncritical of signals and demands.[44] There seems to be general agreement that in the state of post-hypnotic suggestion following trance the subject responds strongly to his unconscious motivations. But people of different degrees of suggestibility will be differently affected by their unconscious. The time during which they will remain under the influence of the hypnotist before the effect wears away also differs. Certainly some persons when placed by the hypnotist in a conflicting situation in which he invokes contradictory impulses—such as gratification of a desire to act and a moral prohibition against doing so—will tend to solve the conflict in a manner characteristic to them in normal life.[45]

It would appear that cases involving a light trance may be dealt with legally as any other case. The nature of the trance would depend, however, on the susceptibility of the person involved to hypnotic influence as well as to the hypnotist. Has the person hypnotized retained control of his behavior?

Are his normal choices available to him or is he unable to handle his unconscious drives? A skilled hypnotist could determine the degree of a person's susceptibility to hypnosis, but the hypnotist's testimony on this subject would have some of the same limitations as that of psychiatrists in cases involving sanity. The variations in depth and boundary of post-hypnotic influences argue against a reliable finding of intent on the part of one who has been hypnotized.

The hypnotic state may affect memory, sometimes creating greater accuracy, but generally causing distortion and a lessening of accurate recall. In a trance perceptions can be altered, hallucinations induced, and inferences multiplied. Just as in normal life we fill gaps in our memory, so a person under hypnosis will create "factual" justifications and explanations of actions induced by the hypnotist. But, as in the case of repression and amnesia, the memory is not irretrievably lost.

It can be restored through release from hypnotic control just as memory in repression and amnesia may be restored through psychotherapy. It would be better in those cases to describe memory as unavailable rather than lost. Insofar as capacity to testify is concerned it would make no difference if it were lost or unavailable. This does not mean that the phenomena of hypnotism, repression, and amnesia are identical; but each limits the amount of content of available data on which choices can be made.

Brainwashing, in which a person is also affected by suggestibility, is another matter. This involves a change in personality which takes place overa considerable period of time and involves the breakdown of the person's original personality, including his system of controls and values.[46] Even if one subjected to brainwashing would come within the *M'Naughten Rules* relative to capacity to distinguish between right and wrong, he would seem not to have a capacity any longer to make a choice. His cognitive processes have become enslaved to the suggestions of his masters.

Both hypnosis and brainwashing may be accompanied by the use of drugs. Some drugs lessen the conscious controls, and, as in the case of hypnosis, "the suggestibility index is heightened."

Hypnotism is not sleep and therefore should not be confused with somnambulism, in which condition one has neither control nor conscious choice.

Acts may be committed while in condition of somnambulism or aphasia, conditions in which the unconscious is in control. The act may arise from the same unconscious drives as when the action is conscious, but it would not be deemed criminal if the fact of somnambulism or aphasia were proven. The capacity to choose is absent.

6. Action Interrelated with Social Transactions

Suggestibility is not only incident to hypnosis and therapy. It is the basis of acculturation, education, law and social order. If each of us lived autonomously, without cooperative needs, in disregard of the needs of others, man, who is the most predatory of animals, would be even more so. For it is the capacity to accept the needs of others as his own and his sensitivity to suggestion of others that makes possible a culture and its legal system.

This sensitivity to suggestion arises out of man's need for support, from the fact that he is not autonomous, that his self-image and sense of social power grow out of his transactions with other men who accept or reject or ignore him depending upon how they value his contribution to their images of themselves and their sense of social power.

Societies can be conceived as individuals and groups held together by transactions which maintain the equilibrium of such groups and individuals. Through these transactions we communicate and receive cues, suggestions as to behavior which will maintain an existing equilibrium or attain a new one.[47] Examples are to be found in the processes of adaptation to the norms of family, peer groups, management, military organization, and government (law).

We are always attempting to maintain balances physiologically and psychologically. This homeostasis* is achieved by chemical processes in the blood stream and stimulation of the nervous system which cause the body to react in such a way as to balance the needs of its various organic parts to meet internal tensions and external stresses. We cannot today draw any established line between homeostatic processes in the physiological and psychological areas. For example, if one is under stress, the body chemistry changes when he feels that he has support.[49] There are further bodily changes that are functions of emotional states, which can be detected by polygraphs, amplifiers, and other instruments.†

Physiological growth initiates a process of change, a reaching out for new experience. From the base of one equilibrium we risk the achievement of a new one. The prone infant has a need to begin to move, to creep, to crawl, and finally to walk and jump. Each of these experiences requires the achievement of a new balance, a further homeostatic platform from which

* Toch and Hastorf, after reviewing various concepts of homeostasis, found two common denominators. The first was that a state of disturbance is followed by a state of relative quiescence. The second was that the achievement of the state of relative quiescence is initiated and is the "object or cause of behavior initiated in connection with" the state of disturbance. "In other words, behavior is seen as ultimately aimed at a state categorized as 'equilibrium.' "[48]

† Behavior can be affected by electrical stimulation of various areas of the brain. It would appear, therefore, that emotional states affect and are affected by electronic processes in the brain.[50]

to try an additional step to attain another value satisfaction. New thresholds are crossed and new values come from the satisfaction or frustration of tensions-needs-motives. We share with many of the lower animals an interest in puzzles and problems, in mental as well as physical exercises. "In summary, then, curiosity, in the most general sense of that term, acts as a motive; that is, it induces purposive behavior which leads either to its satisfaction or to tensions when frustrated." [51]

Thus deviance from social norms may be for the purpose of achieving or maintaining equilibrium, satisfying a homeostatic need; or it may be a risk taken to attain a new experience which becomes the fulcrum of a new balance. *Such deviance is sometimes declared to be criminal behavior or fault, a transaction for which the actor must pay*. But it may also be part of the creative process of scientific, technological, social, political, philosophic, or artistic invention—or just simply escape from routine. As has been illustrated in Chapter II, it is the social, the cultural setting which determines how deviance is viewed. The scientific contributions of Galileo, deviant as they were from the socially acceptable values of his time, came to be regarded as heroically laid foundations to our modern science.

In our interrelationships with other persons and in groups, we are continuously trying to establish balances to maintain our self-image and our sense of social power. We repeatedly test for cues to other's estimates and expectations of us. Often we test, too, how far a relationship can be stretched without injuring or destroying it, thereby perhaps creating in ourselves a sense of imbalance.

If we cease repeated reality testing, which we normally do during wakefulness, "it is easy to drift into a hypnoidal state." This restless reality testing implies that "one is always on the verge of losing his grip on reality, of falling into error, or becoming disoriented." [52]

In each interrelationship we keep asking, as we proceed from transaction to transaction, "How am I doing?" The answer generally sought is approbation, but on the other hand it may be to be rejected and punished. The first process of an infant's acculturation is learning without cognition how to attract attention to his needs and communicate them to others and how to do so in a way which will result in the satisfaction of those needs. This is the motivation for his development of skill in communicating through sounds and motions and later in mastery of the complex symbolism of language. He learns how differences in his behavior result in different reactions by others; that is, he learns to recognize feedback and to alter his behavior in response to this feedback in order to achieve satisfaction of needs. Gradually feedback and adjustment of behavior in response to the reaction of others come into cognition, although never completely. This process is the basis of human interaction, of the transactions between individuals and among people in groups and social institutions. It is fundamental to acculturation, to the absorption of social norms. In other words, we could not exist without suggestibility.

Perception (including feedback), expectation, and wishful thinking* are means to fulfill the need for self-constancy.

* When expectation of satisfaction varies substantially from the probable, from reality, the result is wishful thinking. In this we change, through denial or repression, the mix of the facts to meet a need, or we distort the process by which we select for perception from among the many appearances which it is possible to perceive. Wishful thinking may be considered as a higher degree of unreality than common perception which itself is a best guess or estimate of what we experience. "On the basis of the significances we experience, we are constantly guessing that certain things we do will give us the value-qualities of experience we hope for. We try to repeat many types of activities because they show high promise of recapturing or maintaining certain qualities of experience that have already proved satisfying. Likewise we try to avoid those transactions which we believe will lead to a high degree of negative value-quality. . . ." [53]

They help us to maintain the necessary balance between inner and outer reality which is necessary to healthy psychological life, which makes it possible to be effective in our relations with others, i.e., to achieve our purpose and avoid punishing situations.[54] This homeostasis, this capacity to maintain stability with reference to our environment and conflicting forces within and without ourselves, is dependent upon the feedback we get and our interpretation of it. We are influenced by the cues we get from others. We are subject to their suggestion. Thus suggestibility is not necessarily stimulated by verbal cues or by attempts of others to influence us. A smile, a harsh look, a tone of voice, being ignored, feeling under pressure, feeling dominated or that our aspirations are rejected, perceiving that we are not receiving the same rewards afforded to others though we believe ourselves worthy of them,[55] any of these may feed into us and suggest behavior that will meet our needs.

Our need for self-constancy would appear relevant to those situations in which the question of *intent* is in issue. For intent always involves interaction between the significances assigned by us to our perceptions and our need for self-constancy. In psychological terms they are functions of each other. Intention, then, is the servant of homeostatic need (this need for self-constancy or equilibrium). It is a quasi need-tension, to use Lewin's term, applied to the service of relieving (releasing) a genuine need-tension to support self-constancy. *Thus intention can be said to bring "order into the wide variety of possible action sequences by coordinating them to a final outcome.* Therefore if we are convinced that o did x intentionally, we generally link the x more intimately with the person than if we think that o did x unintentionally."[56]

Groups can influence the perceptions and consequently the expectations and actions of their members. In order to maintain his self-image and sense of social power, an individual will tend to conform to the norms of the group if he does not have appropriate norms of his own.[57]

In his now classic experiment Sherif reported:

> To express the point more generally, we conclude that in the absence of an objective range or scale of stimuli and an externally given reference point or standard, each individual builds up a range of his own and an internal (subjective) reference point within that range, and each successive judgment is given within that range and in relation to that reference point.[58]

Where one has no other external norm for judgment, he will tend to construct his own norm. But where he is sharing experiences with others, there is a tendency to converge on a common norm. The individual will be in a suggestible relationship to their norms. He may not be conscious of this process. "Once the common norm is established, later the separate individuals keep on perceiving it in terms of the frame of reference which was once the norm of the group." [59] Thus there is a carry-over of standards of values experienced in a group setting to other situations which appear similar. The resulting pattern of behavior, even where consciously made, is predetermined to the extent that it is not considered in the context of new experience. It is a fiction to consider such behavior the result of intent based on choice. No choice is apparent to the actor.

If he feels some conflict between a suppressed personal norm and that of his associates or of society, he may say as the dying judge Iván Ilých did: "Maybe I did not live as I ought to have done. . . . But how could that be, when I did everything properly?," that is, "What was considered good by the most highly placed persons," his reference group.[60]

In Asch's experiments, members of the experimental groups

disregarded their own perceptions to accept those which were the consensus of other members of the group. They did so (a) because they decided *their* perception was distorted; (b) because disagreement signified to them that their perception was erroneous; or (c) with conscious intent to conform because deviance might lower their status in the group. Only in the latter case could one properly attribute intent.[61]

This does not mean that all people in all circumstances adopt the norms of their group. The adaptation process is usually unconscious, and where it obtains, limits the freedom of choice. But where one has confidence in his own perceptions; where he feels that he can only deal satisfactorily with a task by relying on his perceptions; or, where his sense of self-constancy sets up an internal conflict with a group or social norm, he may make a conscious choice and intent may come into play. The problem caused by this conflict will be solved through the customary processes where cognitive dissonance occurs.[62]

Merton has shown how prejudice and discrimination are related to different types of persons whose behavior may be affected by social climate. The four types he discusses are:

1. The Unprejudiced Non-Discriminator, or the All-Weather Liberal
2. The Unprejudiced Discriminator, or the Fair-Weather Liberal
3. The Prejudiced Non-Discriminator, or the Fair-Weather Illiberal
4. The Prejudiced Discriminator, or the All-Weather Illiberal

To diagnose the problem, it appears essential to recognize these several types of men, and not to obscure their differences by general allusions to the "gulf between ideals and practice." Some of these men discriminate precisely because their local cultural ideals proclaim the duty of discrimination. Others discriminate only when they find it expedient to do so, just as still others fail to translate their prejudices into active discrimination when *this* proves expedient. It is the existence of these three types of men, in a society traditionally given over to the American creed, who constitute "the racial problem" or "the ethnic problem." Those who practice discrimination are *not* men of one kind. *And because they are not all of a piece, there must be diverse social therapies, each directed at a given type in a given social situation.*[63]

This typology is relevant to a consideration of the problem of intent in crimes evolving from racial or religious conflict. Types II and III are influenced in their behavior by the perceptions and standards of others. In those cases the degree of conscious choice will vary. But in any event the persons involved are subject to suggestion. Their self-image, their need for equilibrium, may cause them to be liberal or illiberal depending upon the situation.

McKeachie has shown that there is a significant correlation between individual attitudes and changes in people's estimates of the norms of the group. His research fortifies Merton's varying interplay between personality and the perception of group norms.[64]

That the effect of suggestion is not always conscious is well illustrated by advertising. Its appeal is largely subliminal or to the preconscious.[65]

As has been pointed out, deviance is frequent. It is necessary to maintain a balance among internal stresses and external stresses. Particularly in situations where formal organization is coercive, deviance or incongruent behavior may be necessary to the individual "to maintain a minimum level of health" and thus may even make it possible for the organization to meet its goals.[66] When conflicting pressures become great, we frequently attempt to escape them by processes such as denial, repression, or other flight, which have already been discussed. These conflicts may cause one "to escape not only from the outer world, *but from one's own patterns*, and the result may be extreme vacillation, of grasping at every straw in the outer world." [67] This vacillation in which choice appears impossible is the cause of many acts of *nonfeasance* in which there is no intention not to act, only an incapacity to act.* When we believe a "reasonable" man would have acted in the circumstances we may even conclude that the vacillator intended *not* to act. This will be discussed in greater detail in Chapter V.

That the influence of a sick culture can have the psychological effect of depriving people of choice and making acceptable what would previously have appeared evil is nowhere more clearly and horribly illustrated than by the effect of the culture of Nazism. The defenses in the trials of Eichmann and other Nazi officials were founded on the theory that they were only obeying the law, that they were influenced, commanded or compelled to exterminate six million Jews and perform other acts by their superiors and the philosophy of the state. Eichmann took the position at his trial that "This was the way things were, this was the new law of the land, based on the Fuehrer's order; whatever he did he did, as far as he could see, as a law abiding citizen. He did his *duty*, as he told the police and the court over and over again; he not only obeyed *orders*, he also obeyed the *law*." [68]

SS Captain Joseph Kramer, testifying at the trial of another Nazi official, concerning people put to death by asphyxiation so that their bodies could be used for "scientific" research, stated:

* Vacillation and nonfeasance may also be symptoms of panic and neurotic conditions devoid of intent.

I had no feelings in carrying out these things because I had received an order to kill eighty inmates in the way I already told you. That, by the way, was the way I was trained.[69]

There was ample evidence in the Eichmann, the Nüremberg, and other Nazi trials that the value system of the defendants incorporated mass murder as an acceptable instrument of the state. Mass murder and genocide were behavior acceptable to the defendants within the norms of their culture.

Bettelheim[70] has pointed out that the greater the threat of an individual's power the greater is the need to deny its evil use "by believing in his virtue." [71] In other words, the power of Hitler and his entourage was so threatening to the individual German, particularly those who held office, that the psychological result would be a denial that anything he and his entourage might do would be evil and the belief in his virtue was illustrated by the passion of his followers.

The inability of men to regulate their lives encouraged the government to control them. This in turn, as Bettelheim points out, reduced their capacity to make their own decisions. This facilitated a cyclical process, necessitating broader controls by the state "which in turn added to the failure of self-regulation" by the individual.[72] In the pathological situation of the concentration camps denial of reality was a step towards developing a means to survive, whereas accepting reality threatened the prisoner's personality integration. It was too dreadful.[73] This pattern obtained, too, among the "free" population whenever there was an impulse to reject the dominant Nazi influence. Reality was denied in order to survive, in order to avoid stress from contesting the terrible power of the Nazi state even within one's self.

Related to this denial of reality was also denial of the consequences of action and the denial of moral values. This was sometimes accomplished by a "business as usual" attitude, by concentrating on skills and the achievements resulting from the use of those skills. Thus a doctor could apply the best techniques for insuring safe childbirth though a half hour later he sent mother and infant to the crematorium. Physicians in Auschwitz could perform the most cruel experiments in the name of "research." [74] It can be assumed that Nazi officials, too, denied reality, consequences and moral values for their own personal integration within the Nazi culture. They could find value and satisfaction in the skills with which they performed their assigned tasks.

Mr. Justice Jackson, who wrote the opinion for the Supreme Court in Morissette (see p. 3) which defined the element of intent in our criminal law, was also the chief United States prosecutor at the Nüremberg trials. In his report of those trials to President Truman he distinguished between defendants of low status who had no choice but to obey orders and those of high rank who had discretion as well as those who volunteered for criminal action.

> There is doubtless a sphere in which the defense of obedience to superior orders should prevail. If a conscripted or enlisted soldier is put on a firing squad he should not be held responsible for the validity of the sentence he carries out. But the case may be greatly altered when one has discretion because of rank or the latitude of his orders. And of course, the defense of superior orders cannot apply in the case of voluntary participation in a criminal or conspiratorial organization, such as the Gestapo or the S.S. An accused should be allowed to show the facts about superior orders. The Tribunal can then be allowed to determine whether they constitute a defense or merely extenuating circumstances, or perhaps carry no weight at all.[75]

In his opening address to the Nüremberg Tribunal Jackson stated:

But none of these men before you acted in minor parts. Each of them was entrusted with broad discretion and exercised great power. Their responsibility is correspondingly great and may not be shifted to that fictional being, the state. . . .[76]

At the Nüremberg Trials (and in the Eichmann trial) guilt was charged "on planned and intended conduct that involves moral as well as legal wrong." "It is not because they [the Nüremberg defendants] yielded to the normal frailties of human beings that we accuse them. It is their abnormal and inhuman conduct that brings them to the bar." [77]

Dinstein in an interesting discussion of one theory of the defense of obedience, *respondeat superior*, criticized Jackson's view that there could be a distinction between lower and higher echelons on the theoretical ground that if the law is to *relieve* an actor under orders from liability "[i]n effect, the decisive factor is not the respective rank . . . but the very obedience to the order." [78]

Furthermore, it would be difficult as a practical matter to draw the line between who were responsible decision makers and who were not. Jackson's distinction between the highest Nazi officials and lower echelons on the basis of the amount of discretion and latitude of orders ignores the pressures which the system put even on high authorities. Roehm was destroyed and high Nazi officials, even SS officers, were sent to concentration camps for having deviant opinions, even without acting on them. (Stalin's purges exemplify a similar process working in the Soviet Union.)

In his discussion Dinstein suggested several possible approaches: (a) the "reasonable man" test, in which a subordinate would be responsible only for following orders which were "manifestly illegal," (b) the *respondeat superior* theory, i.e. that the person giving the orders, not the one ordered, is responsible, (c) imposition of absolute liability to eliminate obedience to orders as a defense; (d) Dinstein himself advocated that obedience should not constitute a defense *per se* but should be considered a factual element that may be taken into account when the defense is lack of *mens rea*. It should be an element similar to compulsion or mistake of fact to negate *mens rea*.* In American law *duress* is an affirmative defense negating *mens rea* and, therefore, guilt, unless a person recklessly or negligently places himself in a situation in which it is probable he will be subject to duress. (Model Penal Code §2.09.) Such recklessness would apply to those members of "conspiratorial organizations" such as the Gestapo and SS to which Jackson referred.

But does not obedience imply that there is coercive power behind the command which operates in varying force as a compulsion or duress? If this be so, command must influence choice of action and, in effect, depending upon the extent of the coercive power, real or imagined, limit the apparent choices available. This is a corollary to the concept that autocratic control reduces the judgmental power and the self-regulating and planning capacities of those controlled.

The assumption in both the Nüremberg and Eichmann trials was that Nazi officials had free will to choose between obedience to the Party Line and punishment by the Nazi police. *Actually free will, choice and intent were not necessary elements to the judgments reached in those cases.* The *intent* of the defendants was irrelevant. This does not mean that even defendants in the lower echelons, not soldiers on a firing squad but officers such as Eichmann, and the concentration camp personnel, should not have been found guilty of murder, tor-

* Dinstein fails to give sufficient weight to cultural factors and their psychological effects.

ture, confiscation and destruction of property. They should have been incarcerated or, if you will, executed for acts which even without intent or choice marked them as dangerous people who could not be permitted to remain at large. The influence of the Nazi value system and the distortions that their cultural norms had performed on them made them unfit to roam freely among other men, although some on the lower levels of the Nazi hierarchy might redeem themselves. (See last chapter, p. 188n.)

The fact that we are subject to suggestion—to influences of various pressures—would indicate once more that there are times when we are not making a free choice but, to maintain our self-image, to live up to our expectations of ourselves and the expectations of others, we accept their values without consciously choosing or even knowing that we have a choice. However, it would not be correct to say that we are deprived of all choice. Many people many times choose to ignore the expectations of others to maintain their sense of integrity, the image they hold of themselves, and their estimate of the image that others hold of them. That is the nub of the difference between the "inner-directed" and the "other-directed" man. But law, as has been shown in the previous chapter, expresses the values of the "inner-directed" man.

As we tend more toward a bureaucratic society, law might well consider whether the degree of freedom of choice is the same today, when the "Puritan conscience" is not so prevalent, as it was in the centuries during which the present concept of intention and free choice developed. For today's major choice, which influences numerous minor choices in our culture, is "between renouncing freedom and individualism, or giving up the material comforts of modern technology and the security of a collective society." [79] Men hesitate, vacillate between these choices, and rationalize that they have not abjured freedom when they submit to bureaucracy and automation. "Unfortunately decision making," from which industrial organization and governments tend to relieve men, "is a function which, like some nerves and muscles, tends to atrophy when it lies fallow." [80]

Hostility

Thus far interaction among people has been principally discussed as though it were for the most part supportive and made for effective communication. But, of course, it is also destructive, hostile, and frequently blocks communication. Crimes, certainly intended crimes, where there is *mens rea*, malice aforethought, present are always hostile acts.

Certain crimes would appear to be the result of group norms. For example: Large-scale police corruption, extensive thefts of merchandise by department store employees, or wanton destruction of property by youth gangs involve acceptances of group norms that are socially deviant in order to avoid rejection by others, i.e., other policemen, salesmen, teenagers. Commonly we attribute such behavior to low morale, but this describes a symptom rather than the disease. Of course, incidents will occur in which individual policemen accept bribes, individual salesmen steal, or individuals perform acts of destruction because of personal psychological deviance from social norms. This they may rationalize by telling themselves that others are corrupt or destructive, thus supporting their self-images by justifying their behavior as conformity to norms.

Common-law felonies and many legislative felonies, as well as misdemeanors and offenses, in addition to being social wrongs in themselves, may be symptoms of hostility. Hostility may be expressed directly as when a man, believing himself a cuckold, slays his wife's paramour; or it may be redirected as when a boy, who hates school and his teacher, rather than attacking a threatening teacher, throws stones through the school window, any school window, or as when society finds a scapegoat.

Self-constancy and an adequate image of one's self necessitate some sense of social power, and hostility has been equated to "the psychological need of power restoration" when the sense of social power has been threatened.[81] Horwitz says, "Since social power represents a fundamental condition for need satisfaction in social situations, reduction of one's power should be phenomenally experienced as an 'attack' on one's ability to function effectively. . . ." Thus hostility may be experienced as "counterattacking" in order to restore one's power which has been threatened or usurped by someone else. This is especially true when one has a sense that the threat to one's power is due to "arbitrariness." [82]

Deutsch has shown that criticism will be differently evaluated depending upon the situation, who the critic is, and what one's expectations are with respect to criticism. He considered criticism given in the family, the school, a work situation, and military service and concluded that "evaluations made by a superordinate to a subordinate are interpreted most favorably, evaluations by a peer next most favorably, evaluations by a subordinate least favorably." [83]

Evidence of hostility may well have probative value that the defendant committed the crime, that he wished to do the injury, that he did it on purpose. But this analysis of the phenomenon of hostility as a means of redressing social power and reestablishing self-constancy would indicate that he may not have intended, i.e., chosen to work the particular injury, or that his perceptions were so distorted by his hostility that he saw no choice.

The sense of loss of social power may come from (1) a realistic appraisal of the situation (loss of job, failure on an examination, age, abandonment of parents by their grown children); (2) judgmental criticism (of a humiliating character or critical of intelligence, capacity, or physical condition); (3) inability to judge one's own worth, self-belittlement, failure to make a realistic appraisal of self (not "I failed to do this" but "I'm a failure"); and (4) failure to meet cultural norms (success measured by money-making success).

Bigness and bureaucracy work for the belittlement of the individual. For the sake of reestablishing his sense of social power and his mental health, man needs to identify with others—other-directedness, identification—he requires their support. This may explain De Tocqueville's description of us as a nation of joiners. Joining, obtaining the support of others, may not completely redress the balance of social power. It may only increase the capacity to attempt to redress this balance through collaboration in hostility.

We see this situation result in crimes related to the current civil rights struggle. Both the Negroes and the segregationists (whose dominance has heretofore not been effectively challenged) have resorted to violence to restore or develop a sense of social power. In such a struggle Merton's "Fair-Weather Liberals" and "Fair-Weather Illiberals" determine the social context of norms, that is, whether a chosen, intended form of behavior is in line with acceptable behavior. We have seen the murderers of fighters for civil rights in Mississippi either not apprehended or, even when indicted and tried, not convicted by a jury. In other words there appear to be situations in which even murder may be acceptable in terms of locally or temporally prevailing social norms. Though the crime is in the statutes, the evil intention conforms to a socially acceptable choice, supported by the prevailing norms of the segregationists' reference group. (I am, of course, not suggesting that this is morally sound or acceptable as a legal norm.)[84] Consequently, behavior may be socially suggested to be "correct" even though it conflicts with another value judgment printed in the laws of the jurisdiction.

We are constantly checking our perceptions, our expectations, and our value judgments, testing them, much as the scientist tests his, against external evidence. We are in this way attempting to assure balance, biological and physiological equilibrium, and homeostasis, as the scientist tries to find balance and consistency among phenomena. In this search for self-constancy we are asking ourselves, unconsciously probably more often than consciously, "Am I doing the right thing?" or more accurately, "Am I doing what is expected of me?" Because of this human uncertainty we are ready for suggestion from those whose support we need—in the family, from peers, superordinates, subordinates, or those whose values we want to accept. Our intention may not, therefore, be dependent on a choice between socially decreed norms of right and wrong, but on how we can best achieve balance between our inner needs and our need for support from a reference group. This may not be a conscious choice, and if it is not we rationalize it as though it were. In law it may be a situation in which conscious intent is presumed because a reasonable man would foresee the consequences.

7. Presumption That a Man Acted with Foresight as to Consequences

"The test of foresight," Holmes wrote, "is not what this

very criminal foresaw but what a man of reasonable prudence would have foreseen." [85] Here again we have a legal test based on *generic* man, a reasonably prudent man, not on *a* specific individual, the "very criminal" at the bar. True, Holmes was not referring to a reasonably prudent man in abstract circumstances. The foresight required "depends on what is known at the moment of choosing." "So far then as criminal liability is founded upon wrong-doing in any sense, and so far as the threats and punishments of the law are intended to deter men from bringing about various harmful results, they must be confined to cases where circumstances making the conduct dangerous were known." [86] Assuming that a man who does not foresee what a reasonably prudent man might well have foreseen should be held responsible for his act by the State or in a civil action by the person injured, nevertheless, it is not at all clear that a guilty choice on the part of the wrongdoer is involved. Were the "circumstances making the conduct dangerous . . . known," or was it that they *should* have been known?

Reasonable prudence, what is to be foreseen, must almost always be learned. It involves an expectation which, like all expectations, is sired by experience. A ricochet from a shot might kill someone, and this might be a reasonably expected result of shooting in a street. It is noteworthy that policemen have to be taught the danger of shooting at a suspect or criminal when a miss might result in a ricochet that would kill an innocent bystander. Here we have a group of people especially selected to enforce law, presumably reasonable people with reasonably prudent foresight, requiring instruction in what reasonable people ought to foresee. It reminds one of Aubrey Menen's primitive boys who had to be taught by a European how to do primitive art.[87]

Of the various fictional characters of the law, the reasonable man is the most abnormal fellow. He has obviously never been in love, never lost his temper, or been in any great passion. He probably stole a peppercorn in his youth but he grew up to be a prig, unloved and unrespected, a behavioral model of the law but not for the acculturation of the young. On the other hand, John and Jane Doe and Richard and Jane Roe, also fictional characters, are much more human than the reasonable man. One's mind can fit them into incidents or clothe them with personalities. One could imagine them playing bridge together or participating in a car pool and being "reasonable" beings who rationalize their way through life. But not the reasonable man. He is something of a stick or a scapegoat for the Puritan conscience or a spook whose presence is discovered even when he is not there.

One thing that makes a man reasonable at law is that he perceives what may be reasonably expected as the result of his acts. He is presumed to have foresight, to be a look-before-you-leap kind of fellow.[88] This is surely a useful expectation to have in everyday affairs. Yet we know and say that people are repeatedly speaking or doing something "without thinking." When people are under stress they are less likely to act with reference to some reasonably expected result.[89] And the greater the stress—as when it reaches a state of terror—the more the presumption of reasonable expectation or foresight loses all reality.

One might assume that having had a previous experience of the same kind a person should be forewarned of the consequences of an act, he should learn by experience. The common law gave a first bite to dogs before the owner was held responsible.* One may accept, too, that experience is the best

* Compare Exodus 21:35 and Mishnah *Baba Qamma* 1:4, which restricted the liability of the owner of a goring ox to "payment of half the damage" for the first three offenses.

—probably the only—teacher. But we do not learn equally from experience, and memory is neither certain nor uniform in its uncertainties. Contrary to what one might expect, for example, "Under conditions favoring involvement in the tasks, those with high drive for achievement remembered more of the incompleted tasks than those with low drive for achievement." [90] That people with low achievement may not learn from previous failure experiences (or wrongdoing) and thus fail to know the "circumstances making the conduct dangerous" is not to be dismissed. Motivation is necessary to learning, though the motive need not be conscious.

When the law says that a man must be expected to foresee the results of his acts, it is ignoring that what he foresees as well as what he sees are functions of his experience and expectations. What he sees, foresees, or doesn't may be a function of his rational and irrational fears and anxieties.

The last thing in the world that a man in a given situation may have is foresight, because if he had foresight he might perceive that he wished to kill and this wish he represses in his unconscious. To foresee the natural consequences of his act would be to recognize that he wanted a consequence which in fact he cannot face.

> The use of defenses prevents the awareness of action tendencies whose expression would create guilt. However, if the need is not strong so there is little or no danger of expressing the action tendency, the person can easily tolerate awareness of it. The strength of the need must exceed a certain threshold to elicit a defensive distortion.[91]

For the same reason he may misjudge the natural consequences of his act. The element of chance in the expectation of the situation is distorted or is completely suppressed. The need and pleasure of immediate tension release obscures foresight of nine months hence.

The legal problem of foresight in relation to choice and intent is illustrated by two cases: Director of Public Prosecution v. Smith,[92] decided by the House of Lords; and Regina v. Smyth[93] decided by the High Court of Australia.

> The conflict of judicial opinion . . . turns on the question whether in proving malice aforethought in murder (and possibly the *mens rea* of many other crimes) it is the subjective or the objective test which should be applied. Stated in another way, the question is whether it must be established beyond reasonable doubt that the accused himself had the criminous intent, or whether it will suffice to prove that an average man similarly situated and acting would have had that intent.[94]

In the Smith case the charge was murder and the question involved was whether there was *mens rea* and intent to inflict serious bodily harm. A police officer suspecting correctly that there were some stolen goods in a car approached the driver's window and instructed him to "pull over." Instead the defendant Smith drove off. There was no running board and the police officer ran with the car, holding on to it. He was dragged along and in the erratic course of the car was eventually thrown in front of oncoming traffic and was killed.

In the case of Smyth, the defendant was accused of murder by striking another person a number of times with a wrench and killing him.

In the Smith case in the House of Lords,

> Their Lordships held that: "The jury must, of course, in such a case as the present make up their minds on the evidence whether the accused was unlawfully and voluntarily doing something to someone. . . . Once, however, the jury are satisfied as to that, it matters not what the accused in fact contemplated as the probable

result or whether he ever contemplated at all, provided he was in law responsible and accountable for his actions, that is, was a man capable of forming an intent, not insane within the M'Naughten Rules and not suffering from diminished responsibility. On the assumption that he is so accountable for his actions, the sole question is whether the unlawful and voluntary act was of such a kind that grievous bodily harm was the natural and probable result. The only test available for this is what the ordinary responsible man would in all the circumstances of the case, have contemplated as the natural and probable result . . . the test of the reasonable man, properly understood, is a simpler criterion. It should present no difficulty to a jury and contains all the necessary ingredients of malice aforethought.[95]

The House of Lords applied an objective test to what *a* reasonable man could have foreseen and intended. If applied to its logical conclusion, it would mean that if a man shoved another and could have foreseen that the assaulted person might fall and fracture his skull and die, he would be guilty of a murder.

Travers and Morris argued that if the principle of that case is sound for murder, it is also sound for any other criminal case:

But whether confined to murder or pervading the criminal law, this decision of the House of Lords merits forceful criticism for it suffers from the fundamental defect that *it blurs the distinction between wickedness and stupidity, which is one of the hallmarks of a mature and humane system of criminal law, and threatens a regression to an earlier stage of development of the criminal law when it was regarded as proper to impute guilty intent rather than to require it to be proved.*[96]

In the Smyth case a subjective test was applied, that is, the High Court of Australia stated its aim to be to determine what the *accused himself* intended.

In this Court disapproval has been expressed on more than one occasion of the use, where a specific intent must be found, of the supposed presumption, conclusive or otherwise, that a man intends the natural, or natural and probable, consequence of his acts. . . .[97]

Travers and Morris consider that the reasonable man test

is a very useful test to be used in determining what was the actual intention of the accused but that it should never be a substitute for proof of that intention. In many cases the reasonable man test will supply the correct answer as to what was the accused's intention but it can never be more than a guide as to what was his real intention. People who find their way into the dock of a criminal court at times have some extraordinarily odd intentions, indeed that is the factor which often leads them to the dock; but it would appear just to consider what was their intention and not what that intention would have been if by chance they had been differently constituted and had been the lawyer's delight, "the reasonable man." [98]

As applied in the Smith case, however, the reasonable man test becomes "identical with an *irrebuttable* presumption that the accused intended the natural (and probable) consequences of his acts. . . ." [99]

There is at least some clarity in making the reasonable man test a rebuttable presumption, however unjust and psychologically nonsensical it may be. But Travers and Morris' suggestion that the reasonable man test is useful in determining actual intention and will in many cases supply the correct answer as to the intent of the accused, but should never be a substitute for proof and can never be more than a guide to real intent, is confusing. Once the reasonable man test is used as *guide* to true intent, the tendency must be to suggest to the triers of fact a standard of judgment which they will find difficult to resist adopting as their conclusion. They will, probably unwittingly, be only too ready to find the expectations of the reasonable man (the man with foresight) to be the expectations of those reasonable men who are hearing the case, that is, themselves. Thus they will tend to identify with the guide, perceive selectively evidence which supports their reasonable man test rather than what relates to the actual intent of the accused.

The same arbitrary doctrine of "foresight" has been the law of most American jurisdictions, by the provision that if one was engaged in a felony and the victim was killed by one of the conspirators, all were guilty of first-degree murder even if not present at the site of the killing.

What Holmes, the House of Lords, and the traditional doctrine of forethought do not appear to recognize is that forethought, like all other cognitive and perceptive processes, is selective. What "reasonable man" A considers a natural and probable consequence of action may not be selected as reasonable and probable by B, whether B be another actor in the same situation or a trier of fact.

In concluding discussion of the Smith and Smyth cases, it should be noted that it may well have been that there was no conscious criminal intent or apparent choice of action in either case. Both cases might in fact come within those situations involving panic or hysteria previously discussed. In any event, even if there were no finding that the specific defendant had no intent to bring about the injury or death of another, he should be held responsible and liable for civil damages; and he might properly be imprisoned (or hospitalized) for his irresponsible conduct, *for his inability to perceive what the natural and probable consequences of his behavior might be*. Thus society might be protected from him or might attempt to cure him of a mental or emotional disorder, but it would not be passing a subjective moral judgment in a case where no moral choice was involved. In the law of torts, liability is frequently imposed for unforeseen and unforeseeable results. Motor vehicle accidents produce "some fantastic consequences"; nevertheless, despite "the impossibility of finding reliable means for distinguishing the foreseeable from the unforeseeable," a man may be held responsible in damages for the injury he did.[100]

The M'Naughten Rules

It will be noted that in the Smith case the House of Lords thought it did not matter whether in fact the accused contemplated what might be the probable result of his act provided he was "not insane within the M'Naughten Rules," that is, provided he was able to form an intent and was "not suffering from diminished responsibility." The *M'Naughten Rules* are the prevailing test for sanity in criminal cases in Anglo-American law. Too much has already been written about that case, which appears to be a strong point defended by those who resist the development and depreciate the values of psychological findings, who are opposed to discarding the *Rules* "from fear that any other test would produce a system 'soft on criminals' and destructive of principles of morality and good order." [101]

Mr. Justice Brennan goes on to say:

> But a glance at the transcripts in more than a handful of cases is enough to convince me that though the accused may be "legally sane"—though he may "know right from wrong"—he was nevertheless seriously disordered at the time of the crime. When one has this experience, he can appreciate why those who would replace the M'Naughten Rules ask: Can a true moral judgment be made about responsibility for any act without delving deeply enough into the actor's background—his biological, psychological

and social circumstances—to attempt to explain the whole man? . . . They [opponents of M'Naughten] summon to their support my colleague Justice Frankfurter who said (in an opinion urging a humane procedural approach to the insanity defense): Man "is not a deodand to be forfeited like a thing in medieval law." [102]

The *M'Naughten Rules* as applied in the Smith case are nothing but an argument to the effect that a sane man not only perceives the difference between right and wrong (and presumably is capable of acting in accordance with such perception at all times) but being aware of this difference it also must be assumed that he is aware of the natural and probable consequences of his acts. Surely we need no psychology to tell us what our common sense and personal experience have demonstrated, that neither our perception of right nor of wrong can always include the natural and probable consequences of our good or evil deeds and that the consequences may turn an unthinking act into *mens rea.* The application of the *M'Naughten Rules* illustrates Martin Buber's description of a fiction being a fetish.[103]

Another relevant rule of the M'Naughten case was that if a defendant "labours under . . . partial delusions only, and is not in other respects insane . . . he must be considered in the same situation as to responsibility as if the facts with respect to which the delusion exists were real." Glueck comments: "Obviously, this is a faulty conception of delusion. It presupposes an insulated logic-tight compartment in which the delusion alone holds sway, leaving the balance of the mind intact and sound." [104]

The *M'Naughten Rules*, it should be clear, are founded on an erroneous hypothesis that behavior is based exclusively on intellectual activity and capacity. Reason is overrated, emotion and unconscious motivation are undervalued. "Actually, in the psychic effort to rationalize forbidden behavior with reality *reason* and *choice* are more often observed in bolder relief *after* the act." [105] The process of choice is attributed by the observer after the act, *post hoc, ergo propter hoc.*

It is rarely considered that although the defendant may know the difference between right and wrong at the time he does injury to another and is therefore legally sane, nevertheless to the psychiatrist he may be mentally ill in that he "committed the offense out of unconscious need of punishment." [106]

A man may know his act to be unlawful and yet be unable to control his behavior. Under the *M'Naughten Rules* he would, nevertheless, be responsible for his behavior.

> Capacity to know the nature and wrongfulness of conduct may not have been discernibly destroyed and yet the transformations in ability to cope with the external world, worked by severe psychosis, may have otherwise destroyed the individual's capacity for self-control. In cases such as this *McNaughten* decrees legal responsibility. But since it is precisely the destruction of capacity for self-control, in consequence of mental disease or defect, which from the point of view of morals and of legal policy warrants the special treatment of the irresponsible, the statute forces a discrimination which is neither logical nor just. We think that the discrimination should be rectified by an amendment of the statute.[107]

The *Rules* are derived from the "wild beast" test pronounced by the English Courts in 1724. According to this prescription, one would not be responsible "if he could not distinguish good from evil more than a wild beast." [108] Popular belief, which lawyers and jurists may share emotionally, if not intellectually, even now frequently identifies mental illness with insanity and insanity with wild beasts. The wild beast cannot have intention, but are we not perhaps reluctant to let him live, or at least not to chain him up as was long practiced in mental institutions on those who cheated the gallows?

Dissatisfaction with the *M'Naughten Rules* by psychiatrists, jurists, and legal scholars in this country is well documented by Judge Bazelon in the Durham case.[109] This dissatisfaction led to the development of the irresistible-impulse test as a supplementary test of criminal responsibility.[110] However, the court in the Durham case pointed out that this test "is also inadequate in that it gives no recognition to mental illness characterized by brooding and reflection and so relegates acts caused by such illness to the application of the inadequate right-wrong test."[111] Furthermore, the irresistible impulse might be more difficult to prove than some other expressions of mental disease or mental defect. Consequently, Judge Bazelon adopted a broader rule for the District of Columbia: "It is simply that an accused is not criminally responsible if his unlawful act was the product of mental disease or mental defect." This was a step forward in adjusting law to psychiatry, but most American jurisdictions, as well as those in England, have not been able to free themselves from the tradition of the *Rules*. In any event, as Leifer asserts, the role of the psychiatrist is different under Durham than under M'Naughten.[112] He is in a better position to render his professional opinion under the former.

Without fully adopting the rule of the Durham case, the *Draft of the Model Penal Code*, Section 4.01, has met some of the psychological defects of the *M'Naughten Rules*.[113] However, the *Model Penal Code* includes a limitation to the effect that mental disease or defect, as used in the respective articles, "do not include an abnormality manifested only by repeated criminal or otherwise anti-social conduct." This is difficult to explain. A single act of larceny might not indicate mental illness in terms of lack of capacity to "appreciate the criminality or (wrongfulness) of his conduct or conform his conduct to the requirements of the law." Similarly, a single act of arson might not do so, nor would passing a few bad checks. But it is repeated acts of pilfering or shoplifting, repeated acts of setting fire to buildings or baby carriages, and periodic sprees of passing bad checks which would be the best clinical evidence of kleptomania or pyromania or a compulsion to defraud. In other words, the very repetitive character of deviance may be the best proof of the incapacity "to cope with the external world." The compulsion to repeat an act known to be in violation of social norms, or known to be ineffective to achieve a cognitive goal, is the symptom of neurosis. It would appear, therefore, that the draftsmen of the *Model Penal Code* took away with one hand part of the reform they effected with the other, perhaps because unwittingly they could not free themselves completely from the punitiveness of the *M'Naughten Rules*.[114]

More than the existence of an understanding of right and wrong is involved in determining intention. There is, as has already been shown, the question of whose concept of right and wrong is to be the norm (Chapter II). There is also the consideration of distorted perception arising out of the unconscious, which may involve neuroses. Distortions resulting from such unconscious defenses as repression, projection, and identification with the aggressor are involved. And there are also those distortions resulting from our common fallibility in perceiving, psychological denial of what we perceive, and the influence of our transactions with others—individuals or groups—whose perceptions of objects, persons, and norms may color and distort our own.

8. Conscious Intent

Finally there is the situation in which a person does have the conscious intention to do a wrongful act, and in which he perceives a choice he is capable of making. This does not present a moral problem or one of psychological purpose, but it may well raise psychological questions of evidence such as what are the appearances that cause us to determine that someone else *intended* to behave as he did.

To say that the unconscious makes questionable the legal concept of intention and the legal presumptions of intent does not mean that men should not be held responsible for their actions. It does make a difference, however, whether a man is held responsible for his intended wrongful behavior, done with malice aforethought, by an evil hand, with an evil mind, *mens rea,* or for an act performed without conscious intent, without choice, or the capacity to choose in the circumstances.

The introduction of the concept of intent was a great advance in law. A man could no longer be held responsible for the fortuitous that followed an act of his. From our knowledge of psychology, however, are we not forced back to the humility of the judges who believed that "The thought of man should not be tried, for the devil himself knoweth not the thought of man"? [115] The acts for which society holds a man responsible might be the same, but the punitive response to an act performed with *mens rea* would not be relevant to behavior to which hypothetical intention is now attributed. If we applied a subjective rather than an objective test of guilt, we would be in a better position to apply treatment appropriate to the individual case. A more scientifically experimental penology would then be possible.

IV Effects of Drugs and Blood Chemistry on Intent

"AN OTHERWISE indifferent act" will be criminal, or its degree or punishment will be increased, if it is done intentionally.[1] When we speak of something done with intent, we generally mean that it is done "on purpose." [2] Freedom of will and personal ability to make a choice between right and wrong have been the bases for determining criminality in Anglo-American law. This is derived from our Western cultural past, from the Old Testament and Aristotle.[3] If we *intend* an act, we must choose to do the act. In what circumstances can one have a choice, can one intend?

Law will not regard an act done under external compulsion to have been intended. It must be voluntary. The law will not, however, relieve an actor (unless he is a young child) of responsibility if his behavior is psychologically compulsive or the result of his own self-induced condition (i.e. intoxication) unless "as a result of mental disease or defect he lacks substantial capacity either to appreciate the criminality [wrongfulness] of his conduct or to conform his conduct to the requirements of law." [4] This presents the question, How voluntary, in fact, how intentional, is behavior deemed by law to be voluntary and intentional?

The relationship of drugs—principally alcohol—to intention has long been a consideration of the law. Coke believed that drunkards or anyone who voluntarily deprived himself of his reason could not claim insanity as a defense, and in fact the very act of depriving oneself of reason was an aggravation of the offense, for drunkenness "is a great offense in itself." [5] This is not an uncommon attitude today. We conceive of drunkenness as aggravating an offense committed in that state and often become more punitive, punishing the offense itself *and* the drunkenness. We have not always been consistent in our attitude toward drunkenness. At one time the American Temperance Society, for example, considered the drunkard with compassion and sympathy, at other times he was a "fallen man." [6] It has been pointed out that slow as the world has been to consider as sick the chronic alcoholic, it has been even slower "to concede that the alcoholic does not voluntarily choose the road to ruin." [7] In fact, our traditional attitude is that the drunken man "is something less than human," and if he is an alcoholic he is "socially despised as a member of the deviant community." [8]

When intent in the form of premeditation is an element of a crime, drunkenness, while not absolving a defendant of crime, may reduce the degree of the offense. Thus the Court said in Heideman v. United States:

> Drunkenness is not per se an excuse for crime, but nevertheless it may in many instances be relevant to the issue of intent. One class of cases where drunkenness may be relevant on the issue of intent is the category of crime where specific intent is required. . . . Drunkenness, while efficient to reduce or remove *inhibitions*, does not readily negate *intent*." [9]

We find this concept carried through to the *Model Penal Code* (Section 2.08) where intoxication is not deemed in itself to be mental disease, and is not a defense to criminal action, but may be a defense if "it negatives an element of the offense" (as where premeditation is required).*

Similarly, in civil cases a wrongdoer is not exonerated by reason of his drunkenness. The probability is that, because of our traditional attitude, proof of drunkenness will increase rather than decrease the likelihood of finding the drunkard responsible for his assault or the accident in which he is involved and increase the damages assessed against him. This, in a sense, is a package deal: We punish drunkenness plus the tort or crime committed under its influence.

But what is drunkenness? Is a man who is too drunk to drive, whose motor reactions and perceptions are too far from normal to judge road situations accurately also too drunk to perform some other task? I was associated once with a lawyer who believed he needed a drink in the morning, another at lunch and a third during the afternoon recess to try a case; and thus fueled he did an admirable job. Probably naïve definitions of drunkenness are functions of one's attitude toward alcohol and the culture of a particular community. An example of this is the definition by William C. Ruger, a leading member of the bar in Syracuse, New York, toward the end of the last century, later Chief Judge of the New York Court of Appeals. He used to say: "If a man enters the gate of his front yard, staggers to his door and can't put his key in the lock, he isn't drunk; if he goes through his gate and falls in the grass and can't get up, he isn't drunk; but if he goes through his gate, falls on his lawn, can't get up but puts his key in the lock and opens the door, then he's drunk." Needless to say, he

* When intoxication is *not self-induced* or when it is pathological, so that the actor "lacks substantial capacity either to appreciate" the criminality or wrongfulness of his behavior or is unable to conform his conduct to legal requirement, it becomes an affirmative defense.[10]

would hardly have accepted this definition on the bench.

But how much weight can one place on testimony as to drunkenness? Individual and community value systems undoubtedly affect the attitudes of the triers of fact. The way testimony as to inebriation can be variously interpreted is to be seen by comparing the majority and dissenting opinions in Heideman v. United States, already cited. Perhaps the most reliable evidence is to be had from an analysis of the alcohol level in the blood.[11] Even this would in all probability not be precise evidence because the metabolic processes of people differ.[12]

The idea that self-induced intoxication is itself reprehensible assumes that every man can control his drinking habits and that he has a free choice to abstain. This raises the question of the nature of alcoholism. To psychiatrists and psychologists alcoholism in itself is not a crime. It is an attempt to solve or evade conflicts and their incident anxieties.

Alcoholism is frequently a form of self-destructiveness and an expression of hostility. "When Russian roulette is played with a pistol, the pathology is obvious; when the same game is played with an automobile, the pathology is less obvious but affects more people." [13]

If alcoholism is deemed to be a disease, as the American Medical Association claims,[14] it is a disease that affects intent and, therefore, responsibility for criminal acts. Again this does not mean that the alcoholic should not be responsible in tort law for the damages he has caused or should be left undeterred to commit other destructive acts; but it would seem proper to consider drunkenness as behavior to be dealt with as drunkenness and not as an element of another offense.

Mention has already been made of the anxiety-reducing function of alcohol. Other conditions being equal, the more alcohol consumed the greater will be the anxiety reduction; and conversely there is a direct relationship between the degree of anxiety and the amount of liquor required for its reduction. As behavior which reduces anxiety is rewarding, there will be a tendency to form the habit of drinking where anxiety persists.[15]

Horton has made a cross-cultural study of alcohol in primitive societies.[16] He found that in societies in which alcohol was used there was a high level of anxiety, whether caused by problems of subsistence or authority (in the form of sorcery, the threat of ancestors, or other super-ego configurations). In such situations drunkenness reduced the normal controls over aggression and sexual conduct. Thus, assuming that an inebriated person can perceive a choice of behavior, he may be less able to control his aggressive or sexual drives than if he were sober. For there is a functional relationship between drug consumption and control. Release of controls which may be the causes of anxiety may be the very need served by drugs.

Horton refers to a study of a Northeastern Indian culture in which "emotional restraint, stoicism, fortitude under torture, the inhibition of all expression of aggression in interpersonal relations, a culturally demanded amiability and mildness in the face of provocation to anger, and suppression of all open criticism of one's fellows are typical characteristics." [17] Although in this particular tribe there was an absence of superordinate authority, open conflicts were rare. The inhibited aggressive impulses were constantly being expressed by means of slanderous statements. (We have all seen in our own society the release of aggression through gossip.) Social controls were in a measure obtained through sorcery—the super-ego expression of that culture. Subsistence conditions were serious, continually threatening. When alcohol was introduced to these people they found release from anxiety and repressed hostility in drunkenness, injuring, killing, or endangering the lives of others, even members of their family, and frequently strangling themselves. Destruction of everything in the wigwam was common. Their punishment was through a sense of guilt which, as often happens with alcoholics in our culture, increased anxiety tensions until the next release through alcohol.

It would seem, then, that alcoholism, the most frequent form of drug addiction in our society, can be a compulsive defense against anxiety, and its very compulsive nature denies the existence of freedom of choice to one under its influence. (See Chapter III, pp. 81–83.) Furthermore, there seems to be no doubt that alcohol impairs judgment and "that in the chronic alcoholic disorders of thinking become prominent," [18] the very sources of judgment become inoperative. "The prime action of alcohol in the body is its depressant action on the function of the central nervous system, the brain." Two or three ounces of whiskey will depress the uppermost levels of brain functioning, diminish inhibitions and judgments. They will distort or blunt a person's judgment concerning himself and his behavior, and his relations with others.[19]

Other drugs, such as mescaline, have been found to affect the action of enzymes. An enzyme called amine oxidase combines with adrenalin and destroys it when the emergency calling for the presence of high quantities of adrenalin in the blood has passed. However, as a mescaline molecule has a certain resemblance to adrenalin, the amine oxidase enzyme may attach itself to the mescaline, leaving the adrenalin unreduced in the system; and this can seriously affect brain functioning. The result may be to give a sense of having experiences that are without objective reality. Should we punish a man for crime done under the influence of mescaline and, perhaps, declare the user guilty of an aggravated offense as Coke did regarding alcohol? Or should the user be treated for his illness?

Among hallucinogens must also be included such drugs as LSD (lysergic acid diethylamide), which subjects the blood chemistry of the user to similar malfunctioning. The use of LSD and other hallucinogens deprives the person who takes them of normal perception and reasoning processes. They also deprive him of the capacity to choose, that is, to intend in any realistic sense. While under the effect of these hallucinogens he is in many ways similar to the schizophrenic. Here again there may be no perceived alternative and thus no choices available.

Addictive drugs consumed by man for the most part tend to be depressants or pacifiers, heroin and morphine, for example. In themselves they do not ordinarily lead to criminal action. The crimes of those drug users are usually committed for the purpose of obtaining the drugs they crave.[20] The fact that such crimes may be planned does not make them any less compulsive. That is, there may be a perceived choice of conduct but incapacity to act on any choice that would deprive the user of the drugs he craved. As these crimes would not be necessary to them if the laws permitted the prescription of drugs adequate to maintain users in a condition in which their craving is satisfied, they can be considered to be crimes induced by the law.

Marijuana is not habit-forming. It is exhilarating. It results in loss of inhibitions and a normal sense of time. It is in many ways similar to alcohol in its effects. It does not, however, have the physiological dangers of alcohol for the taker. It has been said that "the accusations that are leveled at marijuana are all applicable to alcohol." [21] The arguments as to the effects of the use of alcohol on perception, mental processes, and freedom of choice and, thus, intention are also applicable to marijuana. Like alcohol, it tends to distort judgment.

The use of drugs may not only result in lowering inhibitions and releasing drives to criminal behavior. Not only may deprivation of habit-forming drugs stimulate criminal acts in order to make it possible to obtain more drugs to satisfy the craving for them. Recent experiments indicate that the threshold of criminality may be directly related to the chemistry of the body without the intervention of drugs.

Schachter and Latané[22] performed several experiments relevant to the problem of intent by manipulating behavior through the use of certain drugs. In the first experiment a group of college girls took an examination. They were told that the experimenter wished to determine the effects of vitamins on perception. Some were given chlorpromazine, a sympathetic depressant, others a placebo pill. Both were administered orally. Among other characteristics, chlorpromazine is "an effective fear-reducing agent." They were told that the grades on the final examination would depend on how they did on this one and that by doing well, they might change a high C grade to an A. While the drug was still effective all subjects were asked to grade themselves on the examination which they had taken, and were given an opportunity to cheat.

Cheating was defined as "deliberate changing of an examination so as to increase the score," as by "erasing or crossing out the answer, or of answering a question that had been left blank." It was found that about forty percent of those who had taken chlorpromazine and upon whom the drug was effective cheated, as compared with about twenty percent of those who had taken the placebo.[23] In other words, those who were under the influence of the drug which was a sympathetic depressant, a fear-reducing agent, cheated twice as often as those who had taken the placebo.

Certain sociopaths in whom "neither neurotic motivation, hereditary taint, nor dissocial nurture" appear determinant were found by Cleckley[24] to have "a lack of normal affective accompaniments of experience." Feeling was lower in them than in normal people. Lykken,[25] basing an experiment on this finding, comparing such sociopaths with normals, found the former to be relatively defective in developing anxiety in response to warning signals previously associated with shock; to indicate "abnormally little *manifest anxiety* in life situations normally conducive" to anxiety response; and to have relative incapacity to learn avoidance "where such learning can only be effected through the mediation of the anxiety response."

In another experiment, Schachter and Latané[26] carried further this line of research. They used epinephrine (adrenalin), a stimulant of the sympathetic nervous system, which governs emotional responses. The subjects of this experiment were sociopaths who were characterized by emotional flatness.

The experiment used inmates of a state penitentiary and a reformatory. They were divided into three groups, only two of which need concern us: One was composed of persons with normal feeling capacity; the other of sociopaths who were chronic misbehavers and lacked affectivity. Some of the characteristics of the latter group were average or superior intelligence, freedom from irrationality "or other symptoms of psychoses," without sense of responsibility, disregard of truth, no sense of shame, antisocial behavior without apparent compunction, inability to learn from experience, general poverty of affect (emotion), lack of genuine insight, little response to special consideration or kindness, weak sex-craving, casual regarding sex.[27] That sociopaths showed less fear than normals is witnessed by the fact that thirty-three percent of them had attempted escape, whereas none of the normals had; and to attempt escape from prison can be assumed to require certain fearlessness, or at least denial of possible consequences. "The experimental device employed measured simultaneously the ability of subjects to learn a 'manifest' positively reinforced task and to learn a 'latent' pain-avoidance task." [28] Immediately prior to beginning to work on the experimental apparatus, some subjects were injected with placebo and the others with epinephrine (adrenalin), a sympathomimetic agent, i.e., its effects with minor exceptions mimic the action of the sympathetic nervous system.[29]

The test apparatus involved "a complicated mental maze" in which there were twenty choice-points "at each of which the subject could advance to the next choice-point only by pressing an arbitrarily correct switch." In addition to the correct switch at each choice-point there were three incorrect, and if any one of these was pressed the machine did not advance and an error accumulated on a counter. At each choice-point one of the three incorrect switches was set arbitrarily to give "a moderately painful electric shock" which was also recorded. A subject would be able to avoid the shock by careful selection; that is, by making a proper choice he could avoid the shock.

At a second session the same pattern was repeated, although the maze had been changed. Those who had received the placebo at the first session were injected with epinephrine the second and those who had received the drug the first time received the placebo the second.

The results were that both normals and sociopaths learned equally well the positively reinforced task. The normals learned well to avoid shock—avoidance learning—but the sociopaths did not. They "seemed virtually incapable of learning to avoid pain when injected with the placebo." However, when they were under the influence of the adrenalin, they were able to learn pain avoidance "dramatically well." On the other hand, normals appeared to be "adversely affected," for with adrenalin they did not learn at all. "Obviously," say Schachter and Latané, "there is a marked interaction between degree of sociopathy and the effects of sympathetic arousal on avoidance-learning ability." [30] This is indicated, too, by the histories of the persons nominated for the experiment by the prison authorities. After dividing them between normals and sociopaths it was found that the latter had committed twice as many crimes as the former. They had not learned from past experience.

If people low in emotional capacity do not learn from painful experiences as readily as normal people, it can be assumed that such deterrents to antisocial conduct as fear of punishment or shame will not tend to restrain them. They lack a physiological factor which normally affects, by inhibiting, socially deviant conduct. Consequently, socially accepted norms of behavior may not be effectively present in their choice field. This is not because they are not normally intelligent. Rather it is because they "appear to be more responsive to every titillating event," whether only mildly provoking or dangerously threatening, than normals, and to feel "no differently during times of danger than during relatively tranquil times." [31] In their own way, these sociopaths are as abnormal in their perceptions and controls as schizophrenics.

The nature of the crimes committed by the two groups is illustrative. The sociopaths had not committed crimes of passion, but "cool" crimes. They were burglars, con men, forgers, and the one murderer "had killed in a well-calculated attempt to collect insurance." It was the normals who had committed assault, rape, and manslaughter, and one committed the murder of "the high school principal who was sleeping with his wife." [32]

A psychiatric study of four men convicted of "bizarre, apparently senseless murders" bears out the unreasoned, seemingly unintentional cruelty of such offenders. Severe corporal punishment was accepted by at least one of them as a phenomenon natural to life. "Guilt, depression and remorse were strikingly absent." They sought as targets for their aggression "innocuous and relatively unknown victims" because of unconscious motivations.[33]

We may conclude, then, that metabolic disturbance produced by the use of drugs (alcohol included) or abnormal endocrine conditioning distorts perception and feeling. People so affected may not be able to perceive available choices or, perceiving them, may be unable to choose or act on a choice. Certainly drug users while under the influence of drugs are not reasonable men who may be presumed to perceive the consequences of their acts. They are at least temporarily sick people who nevertheless may perpetrate the most horrible offenses.* But apart from the ethical problem of punishing sickness (which in itself may be deemed hostility on the part of those inflicting punishment), there is the very real question, What's the use? For threat of punishment, which purposes to restrain intended criminal acts, is ineffective, it will not touch the motivation of people who are physiologically or psychologically immune to normal fear of punishment, who do not feel remorse, or who under the influence of drugs are incapable of

* The federal courts have recently recognized the fact that drug addiction and chronic alcoholism are diseases.[34]

anticipating the consequences of their behavior. They may need medical or psychological treatment, or society may require their isolation even for life, but their *punishment* can only satisfy their need to purge themselves of guilt feelings (as in the case of alcoholics) or assuage the punitiveness of those who determine and enforce the penalties. It is unrealistic to apply the doctrine of *mens rea* to such people. Their intention, lack of intention, or capacity to choose and intend are relevant only to their therapy, not to their guilt.

V The Appearance of Intent

WE HAVE been reviewing the nature of intention as a function of conscious choice, of the unconscious and of social perceptions and values. The ever-present question is, How do those who perceive the behavior of others see intentionality? A finding of guilt or fault depends on the *perceptions* and *inferences* of the triers of fact. Their perceptions are subject to the same limitations as those of any witness. Although a witness too may indulge in inferences, unless he disguises them as perceived facts he is generally not permitted to testify to them. Triers of fact are less limited in their use of inference. It is assumed that a jury or a judge deciding the facts will make inferences deduced from facts in evidence. A case depending upon circumstantial evidence must be determined by inference.*

* *Black's Law Dictionary*, "inference. In the law of evidence. A truth or proposition drawn from another which is supposed or admitted to be true. A process of reasoning by which a fact or proposition sought to be established is deduced as a logical consequence from other facts, or a state of facts, already proved or admitted. . . . A deduction which the reason of the jury makes from the facts proved, without an express direction of law to that effect."

Webster's New World Dictionary of the American Language, "Infer . . . 2. to conclude or decide from something known or assumed; derive by reasoning; draw as a conclusion."

Black's Law Dictionary, *supra*, "circumstantial evidence. . . . inferences drawn from facts proved . . . preponderances of probabilities, . . . process

Inference is similar to expectation, although described in the dictionaries as being the result of processes of logic or reasoning. It is a function of experience, including culture, folklore, literature, and scientific theory, and it is also entwined with fantasy. Like expectation, it involves a probability guess.

By inferring, furthermore, we tend to go through an abstracting process. Hayakawa gives some examples of this and shows how we unconsciously "climb to still higher levels of abstraction." He suggests that John Doe may be introduced as one "who has just been released after three years in the penitentiary." The abstraction then is "John Doe is an *ex-convict* . . . he is a *criminal*." Criminal not only is a higher level of abstraction than the statement that the man had spent three years in a penitentiary, but it is a judgment implying "He has committed a crime in the past and will probably commit more crimes in the future." The law tries to guard against this particular inference by prohibiting the introduction of a defendant's record of prior convictions unless he takes the witness stand, and then admits his record only to challenge his credibility. But do we know, do we believe that evidence admitted for that limited purpose will not influence the determination of the triers of fact on the issue of guilt? Certainly a lawyer, particularly in a criminal case, will try to avoid putting a defendant who has a criminal record on the witness stand, because he believes the jury's inference will go beyond the matter

---

of decision by which court or jury may reason from circumstances known or proved, to establish by inference the principle fact. . . . It means that existence of principal facts is only inferred from circumstances. . . . The proof of various facts or circumstances which usually attend the main fact in dispute, and therefore tend to prove its existence, or to sustain, by their constancy, the hypothesis claimed. Or as otherwise defined, it consists in reasoning from facts which are known or proved to establish such as are conjectured to exist." [1]

of credibility. Perhaps there should be research to determine the extent of such influence.

Another illustration is derived from the spread of rumor. Some people are unable to refrain from going to higher levels of abstractions: reports to inferences to judgments. As a sample of this kind of "reasoning" Hayakawa suggests the following:

Report. "Mary Smith didn't get in until two last Saturday night."

Inference. "I bet she was out tearing around."

Judgment. "She is a worthless hussy. I never did like the looks of her. I knew it the moment I first laid eyes on her." [2]

People can be earnestly trying to find the truth and to reach a just decision without ever being conscious that they are drawing inferences and making judgments in this manner. We can each test this by listening attentively to the flow of conversation in many a social gathering.

The Inference of Intent

If we know what a person wishes to happen, to occur (his motive), and that he has the capacity (the skill, strength, means) to accomplish it, and if he has the opportunity, we infer that he will *try*. Therefore we say he intends to act to bring about the happening, the occurrence, and therefore that he is responsible if it occurs. This is the formula for proving by circumstantial evidence the commission of a crime, and, in a matrimonial case, the commission of adultery. We accept this formula because, based on our experience, it fulfills our expectation of the probabilities.*

Take the Morissette case discussed earlier.[3] The defendant wished to take government property from a government bombing range, he had the capacity to take it, he had the opportunity, he tried and succeeded in taking it (his wish was fulfilled, his act accomplished). For recovery in a tort action no more would have to be shown to establish liability, but the court held that to make his action criminal "a felonious intent," *mens rea*, had to be established. This could not be presumed from his actions, which were open, without concealment, and in the belief—according to his statement—that the property had been abandoned. In other words, for the happening to be criminal, the wish had to be to accomplish something criminal. So in discussing intent we may have wishes of two different characters: one giving a basis for civil liability (the wish to take property not one's own), and another which would support criminal liability as well as civil (taking property with criminal intent).

As was mentioned in Chapter I, courts frequently distinguish between purpose and intent. This can be rephrased in terms of primary and secondary wishes. A person wishes to break a safe and steal the contents. Breaking the safe would be a secondary wish, money the primary, unless to a particular burglar the esthetic (and probably erotic) pleasure of a fine technical job and the excitement of entering an office in the darkness of the night were the principal things he wanted. The law, of course, makes no distinction between these wants,

* Let P represent a person, usually the actor, x a happening or change or a desired happening or change, c capacity to bring about the happening or change, and o the opportunity to do so. We can then express the concept of circumstantial evidence thus: P + wanting x + c + o + x happening, = P tried to bring about x intentionally.

whether primary or secondary. Perjury is always committed for a secondary purpose (perhaps even in the case of a "pathological liar"), sometimes even for a "good" purpose, such as to protect a friend or loved one. If it is found that the defendant committed a forbidden act with a criminal intent, then the behavior was criminal. Whether he acted in order to commit the crime or for some other purpose is not the concern of the law in its finding of guilt. It might be relevant to sentence.

In another place (p. 149) three aspects of trying are discussed: the directional, the quantitative, and the instrumental. We can analyze wanting in a similar way: (1) the change or happening wanted is directional; (2) the intensity of the wanting, which of course is related to the exertion of trying, is quantitative; and (3) the instrumental want represents the means for attaining the primary want (i.e., [1] the change or happening wanted).

Persons accused of crime rarely tell us what they wanted, what their intentions and purposes were, or that they were criminal. In fact we believe pretty generally that people want money, certainly in our culture, and that this want is a motive for crime. It may be that it will be shown in a specific situation that a man who is accused of having falsified the records of the bank and embezzled had just been losing large sums of money at the racetrack and needed the money or that someone was blackmailing him and he had to get cash quickly. These needs, when they are before us, tend to make us believe that the man wanted money and had a motive therefore for his act of embezzlement. Generally, however, as will be further discussed, the inference of intent and the inference of want are based upon evidence of actions, opportunities for action, and an attempt, a trying to accomplish or not accomplish something.

In the absence of specific evidence, what further inferences do we make about wanting and intending? What do we infer and what judgment do we make regarding intention if one or more of these factors in our formula is absent?

Suppose that someone wanting something, a change, to occur and having the capacity and opportunity, he did *not* try to bring it about. Can we then expect he intended it to happen? Or that he was responsible for it if it did occur? A case based on circumstantial evidence infers that he *tried* and that no other force intervened to fulfill his wish. In other words, the circumstantial evidence formula is based on two inferences: (1) the person tried to bring about the occurrence, the change, and (2) he was the effective cause of it if it occurred. If the circumstantial evidence makes out a *prima facie* case, he then has the burden of contradicting the inferences that tie him, intending the occurrence, to the occurrence itself, or of proving that he never tried; or that some other force intervened, or both of these defenses. Whether he tried or did not try is, therefore, a necessary finding in terms of fact though in reality it may be an inference.

Here the law posits its reasonable man as the trier of fact. It assumes he could find that the actor had tried and was the effective cause of what happened unless the latter raised a reasonable doubt as to his responsibility by affirmative proof to the contrary. The difficulty with the expectations of the reasonable man who tries the facts is that his expectations, of course, color his perception. His expectations are what the psychologist would call functions of his perceptions. We perceive in large measure what we expect to perceive. *So what the law is really saying is that the average man's expectations lead not to accurate perceptions of objective reality but to inferences of probable reality. It is on such* "As If" *hypotheses that we then base judgments.* Should lawyers not try to discover more about the relationship of expectation to perception in the trial process?

Let us consider some examples of other inferences on which we judge others. There is evidence that Peter wishes something to happen or change, say the death of Joseph. Peter has bought a bottle of arsenic, thus capacity exists, the means to accomplish Joseph's death. Peter is alone in the house of Joseph, so the opportunity exists. Joseph dies of arsenic poisoning, i.e., the wished for happening has occurred. We infer then that Peter tried to accomplish Joseph's death, that Joseph did not poison himself, and no one other than Peter poisoned him. "It is in this sense that 'can' and 'want' " may be "viewed as conditions of successful action." [4] Therefore we judge that the probability is that Peter was responsible for Joseph's death, that he murdered Joseph. Even if there was no direct evidence Peter wished Joseph to die, we might infer it and come to the same judgment on the basis of circumstantial evidence. But suppose (there being again no direct evidence Peter wished Joseph's death) Peter was Joseph's physician. We then might conclude that he had been criminally negligent, or even reckless, but not assume that he wished and tried or intended to kill Joseph.

Now suppose Peter wishes sexual relations with Winnie, a married woman. Peter and Winnie occupy the same room, so opportunity exists. We infer not only that Peter intended *but also tried* to fulfill his wish, and that he had the capacity, i.e., was potent, and then we infer that he succeeded, that he committed adultery. As has been noted, sex cases are particularly areas in which we project our impulses on others. Our wishes, suppressed or repressed, may become the experiential material which raises the expectation that others have done what we would do if we could.

But suppose we know that Peter was ninety years old, or that Winnie was his mother (theories of Oedipus complex not withstanding), our expectations and therefore inferences would probably not lead to the conclusion of adultery.

If we know that a businessman wished to have a law changed and that he played golf frequently with a powerful legislator, i.e., there is the opportunity, and the desired change occurred, we would not without further evidence infer that the businessman bribed the legislator though he had the money to do so, i.e., capacity and opportunity to do so. The element of *trying* would be missing and not inferred.

In the deep South, where white women have claimed to have been raped by Negroes, the assumptions by the white population include the wish, the capacity and trying, if the opportunity was present. The formula would be Negro + white woman + opportunity = rape.

We see then that the situation determines in considerable measure the expectations we may have and the inferences and judgments we may make as to how others would behave. It could scarcely be otherwise, for man, reasonable or otherwise, is a construct of the experience, expectations, inferences, and judgments of those who project their perceptions of their own reasonableness on him. We see another aspect of this in role adaptation. Our adaptation to a role is a combination of our own expectations of how we should behave in the particular role and the expectation of others as to how that role should be fulfilled.[5]

In addition to the processes of inference, abstraction, and reasoning, what else is put into inference and judgment of guilt or fault?

Intention without an act involves neither crime nor responsibility. On the other hand, "The act is not enough by itself.

An act, it is true, imports intention in a certain sense. It is a muscular contraction, and something more. A spasm is not an act. The contraction of the muscles must be willed." [6] Action, however, may cause the *inference* that it was intended and, therefore, that it amounted to behavior for which the actor should be held responsible. But in reality this action may have occurred without any intent in the legal sense, that is, conscious intention. It might have been random, reflexive, or in panic; or it could have been caused by unconscious or subconscious intent. The unconscious is a phenomenon with which the law has no traffic—at least not intentionally.

However, Alexander and Staub, in discussing mistakes, point out:

> The sin of omission is of great importance to reality, for unlike the dream, symptom, or daydream, a slip may carry with it serious consequences. It is supposed that the law punishes only the bad mistakes, which are the result of carelessness (lack of attention), but the real punishment is at times severer than simple lack of attention warrants. It appears clear that people feel the unconscious intention of the careless person and they react affectively in a manner as if they actually wish to strike at this unconscious trend, by means of severe punishment. In other words, the unconscious of the criminal is taken into account. . . .[7]

To be fulfilled, an intention requires the conjunction of personal (internal) and environmental (external) forces. It may fail of fulfillment because of lack of power, skill, or sufficient motive, or because of superior environmental forces working against the success of the intention.

P can cause x to happen, as by standing on a board and causing it to break, and the standing or breaking may be either intentional or unintentional. Holmes illustrates how an act could be either intentional or unintentional by the example that the same forefinger may be crooked with the same force but the surrounding circumstances of a cocked and loaded pistol being next to the finger makes the difference. "Hence, it is no sufficient foundation for liability, on any sound principle, that the proximate cause of loss was an act." [8]

Commonly, people understand something to be done with intent if it is done "on purpose," that is to say, if it is done with a purpose. But can any act be done without a purpose, without a tension-need-motive?

> The act itself is never the purpose but only the means to the purpose. . . . The purpose may be directed either upon the effect which the action produces *during* the act of its undertaking, or upon the effect which it produces *after* the termination of the act. Whoever drinks water because he is thirsty, or takes a business trip, is concerned with that which lies beyond the drinking or beyond the trip. But if a person drinks wine for the sake of the enjoyment, or takes a pleasure trip, he intends that which lies in the action.[9]

When one steps on a board and breaks it with or without the intention to do so, an observer may in either case express this happening by saying "He did it" as a shorthand for "It was the weight of his body that caused the board to break." But as has already been noted (p. 141), man plus happening, i.e., P + x, does not equal intent, for there may be no act or capacity to choose. Heider asserts that "unless intention ties together the cause-effect-relations" there is not "a case of true personal causality." [10] Holmes and Jackson have already been cited to the same effect. This conclusion on the one hand would ignore unconscious motives and intentions and on the other hand negligence and acts as to which one could reasonably anticipate the results. Intent may change the nature of the personal implication and moral value attributed to causality, but its absence certainly does not eliminate personal causality.

Though the purpose may not be apparent to the observer, the act may be perceived as purposeful and intentional. A man may cross a street because he is in the habit of crossing that street when in fact his intention had been not to cross but to go to some other place. Suddenly he turns and recrosses. Would an act out of habit be intentional? The man might say that he had "changed his mind" or his intention. This problem cannot be solved without reference to the unconscious. What has occurred is that a conflicting purpose of greater weight has induced a change of behavior. A new stimulus might have aroused a new need to be satisfied or called up for instant satisfaction a need whose satisfaction had been postponed. Thus as he crossed the street the man might have become aware that he had just passed his bank where later in the day he had intended to cash a check; but why not do it now that he was there? Thus the tension to satisfy the need which had caused him to cross the street was reduced. Its satisfaction could be postponed for that of another need that could conveniently be satisfied immediately.

It will not suffice to explain faulty acts, such as forgetting intentions, by attributing them to lack of intention. Intention, as Freud uses the term, "is an impulse for action which has already found approbation, but whose execution is postponed for a suitable occasion." This *postponed* execution of intention is another phase of intention. Some change may occur internally or externally which, in the interval between framing the intent and transforming it into motor activity, will "prevent the intention from coming into execution." In this situation the intent is revised or omitted because of the intervention of a new motive, but it is not forgotten. *Forgetting*, on the other hand, according to Freud, is "founded on a motive of displeasure." [11] In other words, a conflict of motives can be resolved by the repression of an intent which might, if executed or retained in consciousness, result in a painful dissonance.[12]

Obviously, we seldom if ever do anything just for the sake of doing it. We act because we expect certain value-satisfactions or because the performance of that particular act will, we expect, lead to some greater satisfaction. "Thus, a multiplicity of purposes, establishing sub-goals in relation to achievements in the more distant future, is operative in most occasions of living." [13] Holmes makes the same point. "Intent, however, is perfectly consistent with the harm being regarded as such, and being wished only as a means to something else." [14] This is consistent with the theory of primary and secondary wishes discussed above (pp. 138–139).

Capacity is related not only to physical and mental abilities and skills, but it is also a function of self-confidence, of self-constancy, and "there is ample clinical evidence that even so stable a characteristic as a person's abilities may be grossly and permanently affected by attitudes of self-confidence." [15] Thus a defendant may because of his training or physical stature appear to have the capacity to commit the act of which he is accused but lack the self-confidence necessary to crack a safe, assault, or defraud. *The rules of evidence and trial procedures are far too insensitive to measure reliably a party's self-confidence and its limitation of his capacity*. This is not to say that rules and procedures adequate to measure self-confidence and its relation to effective capacity are impossible, but to discover them challenges lawyers to research and experiment in ways they do not now practice. In any event, our incapacity to measure the variable of self-confidence again makes questionable the trial process by which we attempt to determine intent.

If a person wishes a particular change to occur and thinks he can accomplish it, "he is apt to attempt it." Therefore *can* and *want* may be conditions of *try*. *He tried* "is often instigated by a wish force." Thus *can* may influence the act by influencing motive, the wish. We know from our own experience that frequently we want to do something because we feel able to do so. And we may not want to do something because we feel incapable of doing it. Looking at others, we may infer that if they *can* do a certain thing they must *want* to do it if they have the opportunity. But the event may never occur. An example has already been given in the case of a charge of adultery. Just because a man *can* steal from the till or shoot someone, it does not follow that he wants to do either. We may say, therefore, that *can* + *tried* are conditions of intent. But *can* + *want* are not necessarily conditions of intent.

If we believe that someone acted intentionally, we generally connect the act more intimately with him than if we believe that he did it unintentionally. We are inclined to hold someone else responsible if it happened accidentally or if we believe it occurred because the actor was stupid, clumsy, acted reflexively rather than reflectively, behaved under stress, hypnosis, the influence of authority or of group pressures.[16] "People are held responsible for their intentions and exertions but not so strictly for their abilities." [17] If a man tries but cannot succeed he is not believed to be at fault or responsible. If, however, he *attempts* to commit a crime he may be held responsible, even though he did not have the capacity to commit the crime. (In fact, the very reason that act was an *attempt* and not the crime intended may have been lack of capacity.) But we would not expect or wish anyone to be so severely punished if he tried but had not had the capacity to succeed. Thus the attempted crime is not punished so severely as the completed crime.

The more we feel something external, *environment*, affected a man's behavior, the less we tend to hold him responsible. Examples would be if Peter slipped on the ice and knocked down Oscar, who broke his arm; or George while aiming a gun or blackmailing Peter required him to do an unlawful act.* Thus we can say that we commonly apply a different measure of responsibility where outside forces affect behavior.

At a more primitive level, a man is deemed responsible for anything he caused, whenever *he* is a necessary condition for the happening, "even though he could not have foreseen the outcome, however cautiously he had proceeded."[18] (See Chapter I.) The concept of intentionality is on a higher level of sophistication and moral values. It is a result of acculturation. We learn the concept of intentionality. This is shown by findings that there is substantial development in the application of the concept of intentionality throughout the age range of eleven to seventeen.[19]

It is probable that all triers of fact have not developed the same capacity to distinguish between intentional and unintentional behavior and some may be more ready than others to judge guilt from the fact that a man caused a specific happening and then to draw inferences of intent supporting such a judgment. It appears that the tendency to draw inferences is inversely related to the amount of education people have had.[20]

If we believe that someone intentionally caused an event to happen—as by stepping on a board and breaking it—we say that "he tried." If, on the other hand, we do not believe that

* But we do not *always* accept as a defense that George influenced or commanded Peter to do an unlawful act. An example of this is the Eichmann case, in which Eichmann attempted to avoid responsibilty for sending thousands of Jews to Hitler's death camps by asserting that he was only obeying orders of his superiors. (This has been more fully discussed in Chapter III).

he *tried*, we are not likely to believe that he acted intentionally. *Therefore perception or inference of trying is an important element of the judgment "he intended to do it" or "he did it with malice aforethought."*

Trying has three aspects: the directional, the quantitative, and the instrumental. The directional raises the question what is a man trying to do, what is he intending. The quantitative raises the question of the amount of his exertion or effort: "How hard is he trying to do it?" [21] The amount of P's exertion may itself be evidence of the strength of his intention, a measure of his expectation of success. It will be indicative of the predominant force among his conflicting motivations. The quantitative aspect of trying is evidence therefore of P's wishing, of his intending, to cause x to happen. If we do not perceive P trying very hard, we may infer that he might have had an impulse to act but had no intention to do so. He may have aimed his gun and then rested it on the ground.

In addition to the directional and quantitative aspects of trying, i.e., what a man is trying to do and how hard he tries, there is the question of *how* he tries, an instrumental question. He may be guilty of robbery when he uses a cap pistol to threaten a bank clerk, but certainly he will not be guilty of attempted murder. The cap pistol could be instrumental to commission of the first but not of the second crime. However, the *how* of trying may be evidence of the *what* of trying. Thus if a dealer discusses a security with a prospective customer and gives him statistical data about the company involved and expresses his faith in the company's future, he would be deemed to be selling fairly even if he proved to be overoptimistic. But if the dealer gave false statistical data and represented the company's future to be excellent when he knew it was financially unsound, he would be deemed to be trying to commit a fraud. His dishonesty would be instrumental, and evidence that he was trying to defraud.

If we know Peter is trying to accomplish something, i.e., effect some change, then we conclude he wants, intends to effect, that change. If in addition he *can* accomplish it (has the necessary power or skill or knowledge and the necessary opportunity), then we expect him to accomplish it; and if the tried-for event occurs, Peter will be judged liable or guilty, as the case may be. If he aims his loaded gun at Oscar, he has the ability to kill him. If he shoots we infer that he tried to kill Oscar, and intended to kill him. If Oscar is in fact shot we are not likely to look further than Peter as the cause.*

Heider points out that one may *try*, not only because one *wants*, but also because one *ought*.[22] This was what happened in the famous case of Bardell v. Pickwick. The reader will recall that Mr. Pickwick put his arm around the widow Bardell to keep her from falling in a fainting fit. He held her because he *ought*, not because he *wanted*. This unhappy bit of evidence was presented to the jury as a *wanted* act (or perhaps wanton behavior) and the jury returned a verdict against Mr. Pickwick.

Furthermore, one may *wish without trying*, as where one either (1) lacks the competence to accomplish x; or (2) lacking self-confidence believes he has not the competence; or (3) just has not the "vaguest notion of what particular behavior will accomplish it."

Because a person effects a change, it does not of course necessarily mean that the act was intentional. It may have been the result of *chance*, of accident; but it may be perceived by another as intentional because of his own expectation. To put this another way, the other person's experience may lead him

* This can be expressed: P tries, $+ c \rightarrow x, \therefore$ P intended $x =$ P's guilt.

to expect, and then conclude, that *can* + *tried* implies the result. Therefore, if we have can + outcome "we often infer" tried, and this leads to the inference that the act was intended. If, however, we have *can, without* the event occurring, we infer *not tried*—that one who could steal or assault made no attempt to do so. This, of course, may be erroneous. He may have tried but failed, or not tried hard enough. This mistaken inference of trying may again be based on expectations, as in the case of the good bowler who made a bad score and who was said to have had "bad luck," whereas the poor bowler who made a good score was said to have had "luck." [23]

When Peter is perceived to be capable of helping Oscar (*can* help Oscar) but does not, it may be inferred that Peter did not try. This may not necessarily be so. For "his efforts, for instance, may have been rebuffed"; or Peter may not believe he ought to assist Oscar as he might be rebuffed, or he may believe it better for Oscar to do it himself or that it is none of his business to intervene. But a witness or a trier of fact might conclude that Peter has no wish to help Oscar. Here Peter *can* plus Peter *does not* help results is an inference that Peter does not try to help or even wish to help. This concept is, of course, relevant to cases of *nonfeasance*. However, if Peter does not try "we cannot conclude anything about his ability." [24]

But suppose Peter tried and failed—then our inference tends to be that he *cannot*. He is not at fault, for he lacked capacity, or some situational force made his trial fail. However, the failure may have been because a new motive had intervened and restrained him. It may have been more the result of the lack of force of his intention than of his ability due to a conflict among his tension-needs-motives. This we are not usually in a position to perceive or judge accurately.

A man's motives may be ascribed to his *environment*, not only to him: "It's not his fault. . . . He has been provoked. . . ." [25] We sometimes say "He did not know any better," etc. The defenses of self-defense and mental incapacity are based on a recognition of this common response to a perception of faultlessness. Juries frequently find a defendant not guilty, or if guilty courts penalize him less severely for a crime of "passion," as in the case of assault on or murder of an adulterous spouse and his or her paramour. In such circumstances, even without legal authority, we may equate provocation with lack of fault, or lesser fault.[26]

Today there is a tendency to excuse deviation because of the deviant's social conditioning or situation. What is an *explanation* of his behavior may be transformed into an *excuse* for it, such as "What are you to expect from a poverty-stricken broken home where there is not even a book in the house and other members of the family have served time in jail?" * This is tantamount to justifying the result by the cause. It is an attempt, often unconscious, to ameliorate the severity of fault liability and the *mens rea* doctrine. It is a recognition that a single standard may not be fair. It is an indication that many people today reject the legal implications of behavior. This can result in a lessening of such responsibility as is necessary to maintain social equilibrium—as well as personal. This growing tendency to excuse behavior is similar to the practices of

* The folly of such a sentimental attitude was expressed by W. S. Gilbert, in *The Pirates of Penzance*, where Major-General Stanley successfully appealed to the Pirate King:

> Oh, men of dark and dismal fate,
> Forego your cruel employ;
> Have pity on my lonely state—
> I am an orphan boy!

With this sentimentality he saved his daughters from forced marriage to the pirates.

the English courts which by superfine reasoning attempted to evade the severity of the criminal laws which, in any event, lost some of their effectiveness when men preferred to hang, if hang they must, for stealing a sheep as for a goat.

It has been shown (Chapter II) that middle-class and working-class values are not always the same and that the greater use of corporal punishment among the working class and slum populations results in a greater frequency of physical aggression against others. If a child's behavior is regulated by appeals to his sense of guilt, he will tend to express his aggression indirectly. Corporal punishment, on the other hand, tends to cause the child to identify with the attacker and express his aggression directly. Consequently, "the working class tend to express their needs motorically while the middle class tend to favor conceptual outlets." [27] The subcultures of socioeconomic classes, with their differing childrearing practices, influence what their members believe they *can* do and what they *try* to do. It is most unusual for a middle-class teen-ager to engage in a holdup. It is even more unusual for a working-class man or woman to commit a commercial fraud.

Middle-class crimes, therefore, are more intellectual, working-class crimes more violent. (This does not mean, of course, that middle-class people commit no crimes of violence and working-class people never commit "intellectual" crimes.) The suffering from middle-class indirection can be just as hurtful or torturing as a blow with the fist or a club. But the law, which does not hesitate to guess the psychological processes of intentionality, is not as liberal with provision for redress and punishment for mental anguish unless there has also been some physical contact. However, the Illinois and New York courts have recognized a new tort. In the Illinois case Knierim v. Izzo, [28] a woman was permitted to recover damages for mental suffering against the convicted murderer of her husband, who had caused her great anguish by threatening that he would kill her husband.

Naïve Inferences of Triers of Fact

This difference in rearing and consequent difference in style and norms of behavior is not limited to the *commission* of crimes and civil wrongs. It affects also the judgment of triers of fact, who are almost always of the middle class, and the inferences they draw from the evidence. They expect different behavior by those to whom violence is a normal experience than by those who appear to have conscience structures more similar to their own; and as in other situations they are likely to find what they expect.

Kalven and Zeisel in their study of the American jury found evidence that "the jury is often alienated by the unattractiveness of the defendant" and that the use of vile or profane language might affect a jury. In neither instance did they find that such considerations determined the verdict, but that "there is always a considerable link, in the eyes of the jury, between the unattractiveness of the defendant and his credibility" and that "the jury does not give the benefit of the doubt in close cases to those defendants whose behavior it finds offensive." [29]

We tend to attribute to a person qualities, values, and conduct of those with whom he associates. We apply the old saying "Birds of a feather flock together." This may be guilt or innocence by association. It is a primitive psychological reaction frequently expressed in the earliest books of the Bible, which remind us that the sins of the fathers will be visited upon their children for a number of generations. Here guilt was established by birds of a feather nesting together. Gradually, Western culture came to adopt the principle that each person should be held responsible only for his own wrongdoing. But it is not clear that in a trial of several defendants tried jointly for participation in a crime that jury and possibly even judge can free their minds from relating evidence against one defendant to the others and, in such circumstances can distinguish the wrongdoing of one defendant from that of another.

Another difficult psychological problem is when to allow similar facts to be put in evidence as proof of criminal tendencies. Lord Sumner in Rex v. Thompson[30] held that persons who were given to unnatural crimes bore "the hallmark of a specialized and extraordinary class as much as if they carried on their body some physical peculiarity." This may well be true as a generality. Psychoneurotic and psychopathic personalities are as much a part of an individual as is size, color, sex, or scars. The important question is, however, whether this be true of a particular defendant in a particular case. It is certainly the naïve psychological assumption which we frequently accept. Our very suspicion based on a conscious or unconscious expectation that one who has been tagged as a criminal will continue to be a criminal has made it extremely difficult to rehabilitate many exconvicts. But a trial is not a game to be governed by probabilities that the past will or will not be repeated. It is an improper gamble with life and liberty to assume that because one has committed crime A_1 he probably committed crime B_2 because opportunity and capacity existed. Such reasoning assumes that he *tried.* American and English courts have often struggled with this problem. English judges have more or less come to the view adopted in the American Law Institute's *Model Code of Evidence.**

A cause of bias or set against those who express their needs physically may be that those who are more controlled by conscience have had to resolve the conflict between their cultural disapproval of direct action (the motoric expression of need) and their own innate animal desire to express needs violently, physically, rather than conceptually. This conflict resolution is achieved by means of repressing their violent impulses. Therefore there is always the chance that triers of fact will be biased against persons of a different subculture and will infer evil intent by a process of projection.† This can be put in another way: If one has foregone the satisfaction of direct physical aggression—like punching a man who has offended him—he can justify such abstention and support his act (or bias) by punishing those who have found satisfaction in such behavior.

Referring again to Hayakawa's example of the girl who came home late one night, which led to inferences and thus to the judgment that she was known all along to be "a worthless hussy," it is possible to understand that such a judgment would be rewarding to a woman who had not dared such freedom as coming home late or to a man who would like to have enjoyed the company of a hussy late at night but instead had stayed home with his wife.

Sarnoff makes the point that "our ability to perceive others

* "Evidence that a person committed a crime or civil wrong on a specified occasion is inadmissible as tending to prove that he committed a crime or civil wrong on another occasion if, but only if, the evidence is relevant solely as tending to prove his disposition to commit such a crime or civil wrong or to commit crimes or civil wrongs generally." [31]

† This is another subject which should be investigated by lawyers and social scientists jointly.

rests . . . heavily upon the reactions that they evoke in us. . . ." Consequently when they arouse in us motives unacceptable to our consciousness, "we are likely to suffer a lapse in perceptual acuity. For example, we may attribute to others feelings or intentions they do not possess." On the other hand we may fail to perceive those that they do possess.[32] Thus we may perceive in persons charged with wrongdoing wants and intentions which we have repressed in our unconscious but which the evidence stirs up in us. Or our disturbed unconscious, to maintain the repressed state of our motives, may blind us to the innocence of the intent of the person charged.

If someone resolves his conflict between cultural disapproval and his desire for violent motoric expression by acceptance of the cultural norm of behavior on a cognitive level, he may by the process of denial be unable to perceive motoric expression as a choice. He may have a blind spot in this area. Proper people just don't do violence. The act itself, not the intention and the available choices or their lack, is all that counts for him. (The same psychological factors might produce the reverse result in people of a slum culture facing a conflict between the norms of what is culturally approved and middle-class offenses. It is possible, however, that further variables may be involved in their resolution of the conflict. At any rate, as mentioned in Chapter II, it is not the people of the slum who sit in judgment, so this problem need not concern us now.)

Another phenomenon which applies to triers of fact as well as to other witnesses is that the needs of the perceiver help to determine his perception of someone else's intentions. We have "the tendency to see ourselves as the focus of other people's actions." [33]

The perceiver selects from among changes resulting from the action of another person the one that appears most significant to himself. It may not be the one most significant to the actor, that which the actor sought, or that which represented his intent. P's behavior might have brought about change A. This might have implied changes B, C, and D. To P change C might be the one he intended, but to O change B appears the important one because of its physical or psychological effect on him, and he therefore selects B as the change he perceives.[34]

An example is the case of a mother who, believing and stating in her will that her daughter has greater financial need than her son, leaves a larger share of her estate to her daughter. Her daughter-in-law is offended, claiming that the disposition is an implied slap at her. Her need to appear as important or as close to her mother-in-law as the daughter causes her to select an intent that is consonant with that need. The daughter, on the other hand, may perceive the bequest not really as a recognition of her financial need but as a merited reward for her constant attentiveness to her mother.

Causality, which is central to criminal trials and tort actions, also presents difficulty. In a series of experiments Jenkins and Ward found that people are unable to judge correctly that some event is controlled by or, on the other hand, is independent of some other event.[35] This is not only relevant to behavior and its relation to intent. The trier of fact may be unable to determine the relationship of the happening to intent, that is, whether intent was a causative factor or independent of the happening.

The needs of the trier of fact which stimulate the selectivity of his perceptions, inferences, or judgments are not always related to finding cause or intent, or even relevant to the situation. A musician was sued by a wealthy woman in an action for money which she claimed she had loaned him. The defendant and his wife were both well-known musicians and were witnesses for the defense. A young man who was a student of the defendant's wife was also a witness for the defense. There was a hung jury. Questions by counsel after the trial indicated that though the majority were for the defendant the dissenters believed that the defendant's wife had been having illicit relations with her student and this inference was somehow significant—possibly threatening to them—and they selected it as the controlling fact, though no evidence of such a relationship came into the trial directly or by innuendo. In another case a member of a minority group sat on the jury. He perceived the plaintiff as being prejudiced against his minority group. This perception—or misperception—caused him to reject the plaintiff's testimony. He refused to agree to the majority verdict.

As previously noted, we commonly infer that if a person performs an injurious act repeatedly, it must be intentional, although if done only once it might be casual. If a boy throws a stone and it breaks a window of a passing car it might be accidental, but if he continues to throw stones that break car windows we infer that he intends to break car windows—perhaps not to injure persons or property but "just for the hell of it." The more frequently similar acts occur in similar situations the greater is the probability that they are intentional, the greater is the chance that they are not innocently done.[36] On the other hand, the very repetitiveness of deviant behavior—as by the shoplifter, the arsonist, and the rapist—may be evidence that there is no freedom of choice, no intent, but the compulsion of a neurosis.[37]

From a scientific point of view, "chance is merely a euphemism for ignorance. To say an event is determined by chance is to say we do not know how it is determined."[38] Mathematical probability involves measurement and counting and a statement of the result in a fraction between 0 and 1. This raises the question of how accurately we can measure "intensity of belief" or intention in mathematical terms.[39] If the scientist is unable to measure such probabilities, surely the adversary method of court trials will not. This is, then, an example of an *As If* presumption on which we attempt to do justice. But, we may well ask, is justice possible when judgment must be made on probabilities? Is the need to protect society from deviance and threats to social norms more important than certain justice? These are ethical and political problems and what weight will be accorded to each answer will depend upon the norms of the dominant social interests speaking through the courts.

Attitudes and Judgment

As has already been shown, set or attitude interacts with perception and affects it, determines the field of selectivity. Thus if I feel negatively toward P (my set toward him), I shall see his behavior differently than if I feel positively toward him. If I see him perform certain acts of which I approve, I am more likely to feel positively toward him than if I see certain other acts of his toward which I feel negatively. But what I see and hear are certain seeable and audible phenomena selected from a greater number of phenomena in the situation. This selectivity is determined by expectations resulting from my prior experience which affect my perception and set or attitude, and which will support my need for self-constancy.[40] In other words, it requires less disturbance of my perception and cognitive system to bet that what has occurred in my past experience will be repeated.

Murphy defines attitudes as "present dispositions which have developed through a long and complex process" and he says that the more closely attitudes and values are examined the more difficult it is to discover "any essential difference between" them.[41] Values are related to motive, high among which is the support of self-constancy. They "are not imposed on an unready individual but, like all other expressions of motives, are developed by organism-environment interaction. . . ."[42] Attitudes and values, which determine selectivity for judge and juror as well as for witness, derive from the interaction of the individual organism and its environment.

Attitudes and values also relate directly to plausibility. Thus arguments that agree with a person's position will be deemed more plausible and, therefore, are more effective, than arguments which disagree.[43]

To judge an intention the trier of fact comes with perceptions and inferences built of his experience, expectations, and needs. Out of this material come those attitudes, those values, through which the evidence is filtered. It is apparent therefore that the slippage between the intent of the accused and the judgment of the triers of fact could be considerable in spite of their best efforts to be fair. This is why a lawyer in selecting a jury is interested in the background of the talesman to determine his experience and his expectations, which the lawyer would refer to as possible bias.

As has been indicated above in the consideration of Hayakawa's discussion of the progression of rumor from report to inference to judgment, the psychological needs of an individual, as expressed through his attitudes, may lead to distortion.

An example of distortion and how misinformation can be

spread is the following: I noticed in a report of an address given by a state superintendent of schools a reference to moral attitudes of high school students as shown in a survey made in his state. The statement was: "One-third of all Seniors saw nothing wrong with bribes for high school athletes." This was a shocker and in all innocence doubtless the superintendent was trying to arouse his audience. It was something for an audience of educators to remember. It could develop a set, an attitude of distrust, which must reflect in their relations with their students.

I was sufficiently interested to check the data to which the superintendent had referred. It showed not what he had said, but that about a third of the seniors had affirmatively answered the following question: "Just your best guess, do you think *any* of the athletes in your school would accept an attractive sum of money in return for not playing their best?" [emphasis added]. Perhaps they "saw nothing wrong with bribes for high school athletes," but they were not asked about their moral judgment and they answered quite a different question, i.e., whether any athlete would accept a bribe.* This process of finding what you expect, what will fit your need, is an everyday occurrence. It is a fair assumption that it also occurs in the testimony of witnesses and in the transposition of that testimony in the process of perception and recall by triers of fact.

Look for what ye want and ye shall find. In the case of judge and jury this may be no more a free choice, a conscious intent, than in that of a witness.

Deep below consciousness are other forces, the likes and the dislikes, predilections and the prejudices, the complex of instincts

* Compare with *rumor*.[44]

and emotions and habits and convictions, which make the man, whether he be litigant or judge. . . . There has been a certain lack of candor in much of the discussion of the theme, or rather perhaps in the refusal to discuss it, as if judges must lose respect and confidence by the reminder that they are subject to human limitations.[45]

How judge and jury perceive the *limitation of memory* in witnesses is relevant to the value they attribute to a piece of testimony. It may be decisive in a case of perjury. It is not only impossible to remember *all* the facts, but we cannot usually remember accurately the sequence of happenings, the people involved, and their physical relation to each other and their surroundings. When something occurs we are better at recalling action than how people look or what they wear and better at remembering these than recalling the setting of the actors or events. There is slippage in recall a week after the event.[46]

In spite of such empirical evidence we are inclined to believe the witness who gives most detail more than the witness in whose memory there are gaps. We favor him who "tells all." The other witness is withholding evidence or has an unreliable memory. Perhaps he has. On the other hand he may be embroidering less and translating fewer inferences into recalled facts. It must be borne in mind that the practice of advocacy can cause such answers as "I don't know" or "I don't remember" to appear to be lying or lack of candor. To accuse a witness of lying, or indict him for perjury because he cannot testify to a complete and accurate recall may compound the injustice of the appearance. In fact "any claims for total or precise recall should be regarded with equal suspicion, if not with more." [47]

Yet in a court of law if there are discrepancies between the testimonies given by two men about some experience which they have shared, and if it is assumed or ascertainable that the testimony of one is more nearly accurate than is the testimony of the other, the more "correct" set of testimony is used as a measuring rod to test not merely the accuracy but also the veracity of the other man.[48]

In this connection reference should again be made to the inevitable selectivity of perception and recall which in all good faith results in one person seeing one set of phenomena and another person another. Unconscious distortion by selection occurs more frequently than conscious; and it is a difficult and generally impossible task for triers of fact to distinguish between them. For they too unconsciously (although sometimes consciously) are the victims of their own selective perception and recall of witnesses and the evidence.

What makes it all the more difficult for triers of fact to perceive the realities of the case and find subjective rather than objective intent is that consciously or unconsciously they may be trying other cases. They may be making an example of a wrongdoer to warn other intending wrongdoers. Furthermore their purpose can be "not only to suppress the dangerous behavior of men of no morals, but to suppress behavior reflecting competing moralities." [49] To do otherwise might upset their own self-constancy by acknowledging that others' conflicting notions of what is right and normal may be as right and normal as their own.

Johnson points out that "We develop a strong inclination to take for granted whatever is familiar or customary" to ourselves and "to people in the world around us," not any people but those of *our* world, that is, our model of reference persons or groups. "Our notions of what is 'normal' are therefore determined largely by the behavior, beliefs, attitudes, and social conditions which we come to accept as 'right' or natural.' "[50] From these familiar or customary values of what is right and natural and what is wrong and unnatural we derive our inferences which we elevate to judgments.

The written law and precedent may be perceived as a means by which the judge can maintain his own self-constancy as well as support social values. By relying on law he anchors his perceptions and judgments to symbolic abstractions which enable him "to avoid the understanding of the human motive of the crime." [51] By searching for objective intent through fitting a specific crime into legal norms he can satisfy his sense of justice and support his image of himself as one doing justly because he has observed the law. To attempt to discover the reality of subjective intent would be not only more difficult, but because it is almost impossible to do within the format of a trial, it would be unsettling to his sense of self-constancy and his image of his judicial self.

Not that this is always the case. Judges and juries have tempered the law and recast the facts to avoid harsh results. Beard has recalled to us that

> There was plenty of injustice in the old common law, but civilized judges could work wonders with it by a careful selection of cases and a liberal use of independent reasoning.[52]

Williams gives examples of how judges have modified rules of evidence established by Parliament in order to make it possible to conduct a proper defense.[53] Juries may react to intoxication of a defendant by concluding that "it blunts a requisite criminal intent." An example would be where a defendant has taken a car to go joy riding while under the influence of liquor.[54]

The use of technical terms, legal semantics, reinforces the judge (as the use of any professional idiom does to the practitioners of that profession). It is an aid to reducing anxiety, to maintaining homeostasis which might be threatened if other idioms—those of psychology, for example—were substituted. For they might involve concepts the judge had not experienced and might result in consequences he did not want.

It is not so much that those who apply law are engaged in transactions of appearance, like the shadows in Plato's cave, or that we all live in a psychological world of pragmatism or Vaihinger's *Als Ob* (*As If*). This in itself is a reality situation. The evil, and it is an evil, lies in the design of the law and the attitude of lawyers that fail to inquire in an orderly manner how greater reality and justice can be achieved in other ways if other knowledge is utilized.

VI ▣ *The Intendment of Documents*

Intent of Testators, Grantors, Contracting Parties, and Legislators

WITH REFERENCE to documents, we use intent in several different senses. We speak of the intent of a document. We say that a man intends to perform the obligations he has assumed by his contract; that he intends to convey title to a certain piece of property; and that he intends that his estate shall be distributed in accordance with his will. We refer to the "intent of the legislature" (or legislation) and the Constitutional Convention. "Intention is . . . often taken as the equivalent of wish or wanting." [1] In this sense we "intend," that is, want, the other party to a contract (or the grantee of a piece of land with a restrictive covenant) to perform his part of the agreement. We want our executors and trustees to do what we tell them to do in our wills, to do our will. We want the laws we adopt as legislators to be observed. By these usages *intent* becomes an umbrella word covering a variety of meanings.

A legal instrument has no life of its own. *It* can have no more intent than the stones of the courthouse or the statue atop the state capitol. So when we speak of the intent of a document we mean the old term *intendment* defined as: "The construction put upon anything by common law; the true meaning as fixed by law." [2] But what does construction by common law or fixing true meaning by law imply? Is it not that whatever purpose P may have had when he executed the document, if later there is a dispute as to its meaning, a court, or other arbiter, must declare what the "true meaning" is, though in fact it may not have been in the mind of the testator, contracting party or legislator?

This is made clear by many writers on the subject of contracts. Williston speaks of the principle of "manifested mutual assent rather than actual mutual assent" as being the essential element in a contract and states that a mistaken idea by one or another party concerning what was agreed to "will not prevent the formation of a contract." [3] He also says: "It follows that the test of the true interpretation of an offer or acceptance is *not what the party making it thought it meant or intended it to mean, but what a reasonable person in the position of the parties would have thought it meant.*" [4]

When a court determines that a contract affects the public and consequently is to be construed most favorably to the public interest, the court is explicitly no longer seeking the intent of the parties. Thus, though a mortgage may clearly state that on the default of the debt on the due day the mortgaged property shall be forfeited, the mortgagor will nevertheless be permitted to redeem it. This, surely, was not the intent of the mortgagor or mortgagee; but once this principle was incorporated into the law by the courts it might be the expectation of the parties.

To Holmes, "The very office of construction is to work out, from what is expressly said and done, what would have been said with regard to events not definitely before the minds of the parties, if those events had been considered." [5] He also makes the point that "By signing the writing the parties bind themselves to such interpretation as the court may place upon the words and symbols employed by them." [6]

Here again we meet the construct of the reasonable man making a contract or adjudicating its meaning. As in any other situation, the outcome will be influenced by the attitude of the judge.* Each agreement, therefore, and every will, too, contains an unwritten clause that includes obligations or grants which may never have been in the minds of the parties. The intent or intendment of a document, must, therefore, be said to include the meaning which a third party, the court, reads into it, *As If* that meaning were expressly verbalized.

Cockburn, C.J., expressed this principle of constancy as applied by courts in discussing contracts "in which a term is introduced that was intended to be used in one sense by the one party and in another sense by the other. Neither party can avail himself of this misunderstanding of the terms to get rid of the contract; but the court must construe it." [8]

The stability of commercial transactions and the certainty of the disposition of decedents' property require that contracts be fulfilled and estates be settled. This commercial need and this need of inheritors can be compared with the individ-

* Cardozo refers to three possible philosophies of judicial interpretation. (1) He cites Marshall as stating "Judicial power is never exercised for the purpose of giving effect to the will of the judge. . . ." Of this Cardozo comments "It has a lofty sound . . . but it can never be more than partly true." (2) He quotes the French jurist Saleilles, who said "One wills at the beginning the result; one finds the principle afterwards; such is the genesis of all juridical construction." Cardozo himself says that he would not put it so broadly. (3) Nearer the truth, he says, is the statement of Theodore Roosevelt that it is the judges who are the chief lawmakers and that "Every time they interpret contract, property, vested rights, due process of law, liberty, they necessarily enact into law parts of a system of social philosophy; and as such interpretation is fundamental, they give direction to all lawmaking." What Cardozo calls philosophies might be described in psychological terms as belief systems, value systems, or attitudes.[7]

ual's need for self-constancy, and in fact, when met, contribute to the satisfaction of such needs in the individuals concerned.

It would have been more correct for Cockburn to have used the word *expected* or *meant* in place of the word *intended*. But in any event the courts are in a much better position to attempt to find out what the parties expected or meant on the basis of language used and the situation to which it is applied than they are to attempt to discover intent as a fact. For there is less confusion in interpreting language symbols—though their meaning differs from user to user—than to the meaning of behavior.

To permit the avoidance of a contract because of an alleged misunderstanding of a term, except in very special circumstances, would open to uncertainty innumerable commercial transactions. In all good faith, a term may have different meanings to the parties after the passage of time by reason of new experience in changed situations. This wisdom is a reason for the parole evidence rule. The treatment of intendment as if it were intention is a pragmatic solution to the problem of the meaning of parties to a document. It better meets the needs of a society concerned with property rights and commercial transactions, and the needs of the parties involved, than would an attempt to find intention or expectation in fact.

Expectations of a Testator

When we refer to the intention of a testator, are we not referring to his expectation of what other persons will do to distribute his estate? This expectation is compounded of (1) his drive to give his wife, his children, or his cousin certain specified chattels or portions of his land and personalty; (2) his estimate of the desirability of leaving his property to certain persons in specific proportions rather than to others or in different proportions; and (3) his estimate based on the law as he understands it of the probability that his executors and trustees will do with his property what he tells them to do.

A will is not an expression of a testator's purpose to do something but to have someone else do something. When we seek the testator's intent we are looking for the orders, the directions, he is giving for the disposal of his property or the custody of his minor children. His intentional behavior is to be interpreted from the implication, the meaning of his words to others. Those others may be executors, trustees, or judges who with more or less certainty of correctness bet on the meaning of his words.

Where a lawyer draws a will the words used are usually words of art, words that have been given legislative or judicial meaning and have a history, all of which may be foreign to the experience of the testator. They are lawyers' symbols which the attorney believes are a correct interpretation of his client's purposes and which he expects will be so understood by other lawyers, judges, and persons concerned with the estate. The meaning may not be what the testator intended at all. This is especially true of clauses giving powers to trustees. "If that's usual, all right. I don't understand it," the client says, and he, particularly she, does not want to take the time to understand it. There is no intention here in psychological terms except to accept the attorney's assurance that the clauses are usual and have a meaning in law. The testator accepts the world of legal art on faith in his attorney, often knowing well that phrases and devises do not and cannot reach his own meaning, which is a personal feeling.[9]

This is illustrated by the following poem:

LATEST WILL[10]

I, of the City and State of, do declare
This to be my Last Will.
I revoke
All prior Wills and Codicils.

Property real or personal
(Or unreal or impersonal)
Of which I may die
Seized or possessed
Anything to the contrary not-
Withstanding.

In respect of securities
(Ah, security, singular, would be enough),
After aforementioned charities,
Paid to the then living issue of such grandchild
Or, if not then living, to
Per stirpes, not per capita,
If they in their absolute discretion

This ring that pressed my flesh
Indenting it with pearly heaviness
(To whom? To whom? what message will it bring?)
Also the special chain, my intricate gold, both links and clasp.
I do bequeath my fall-out shelter
Two weeks' supply of biscuits
The flask and dregs that it contains
Unto mine enemy to whom I turn the other fist.
As for my kneeling in the violet meadow
As for my breathing in the lilac row

As for my sunny brook my snowy brook my fire's glow
To one I love

Hereunder and hereabove.
First (A) I appoint and (B)
If for any reason fail or cease
(If fail in justice, if cease by inner law, I do despair)
I do decree
Which shall be included in my gross estate.
Some interests are subject to foreign death taxes.
(Are some alien interests thus free?)
All the rest, residue, and remainder of every nature and
kind whatsoever and wheresoever and always necessarily
hereabove
(But how shall I make an inheritance of love?)
As the case may be.

Expectations of Contracting Parties

The intention of a party to a contract can also be described in terms of his expectations concerning what the other parties to the contract will do, that is, his drives, his estimation of the desirability of accomplishing certain results, and the probability that the other parties will do what he wishes them to do. In a contract there is a further factor not present in the case of a testament. For a contracting party *also* intends to perform some act himself (except perhaps in the case of a unilateral contract). His expectations regarding his own intended acts can be analyzed similarly to the analysis of his expectations of the other contracting parties. He expects of himself certain behavior as the price for achieving some purpose—receiving a purchase price, a salary, a house, a car, insurance, an education, a spouse, etc.

In each instance the drive arises out of some need (or is the need itself); a party estimates the desirability of the result and the probability of its achievement. And these are based, in turn, on his experience, experience which includes not only similar previous transactions or interactions in which he has been directly involved, but also those in which he has shared and by which his perceptions have been conditioned because he is part of a culture. This includes his expectation derived from law as he understands it.

The form of a contractual transaction can be described as "the practically compelling dialectics of the purpose" which has been "produced out of the two factors of need and reward." [11] In this context intent is the expectation of realizing a desirable purpose by certain behavior which is the price for achievement of that purpose.

Law is presented with problems when there are disputes concerning the purposes which parties to a contract contemplated or the means to achieve the agreed purposes. Similar problems are raised with regard to the desired purposes and means set forth by a will. What did the contracting parties or the testator want to communicate? What and how was something to be done? In the process of interpretation we are confronted again with the nature of transactional realities. The parties to the contract, executors, or, if a dispute be in litigation, the triers of fact are called upon to interpret and define what has been communicated in terms of symbols arising out of their own experiences. They may try to find meaning in terms of what the situation meant to him who executed the will or contract but at best this will be a guess, a bet based upon the interpreters' own perceptions of a situation. What was reality to the testator or contractor will always be perceived in terms of what is reality to the other parties and the triers of fact. The questions in each case will be to what extent will they be projecting their own realities on to him who executed the document, to what degree will they be serving their own needs for support and security, their own homeostatic needs in reaching a solution, in expressing what has been communicated to them.

But is the intention of the party to the instrument always the important communication for the purpose of interpreting, that is, finding the meaning of the contract?

> In the case of a successful lie the person deceived makes the reference which the deceiver intends he shall, and if we define "meaning" as "that which the speaker intends the listener to refer to" the victim will have interpreted the speaker aright. He will have grasped his meaning.[12]

The communication will have operated as intended. *Puffing* of merchandise was acceptable to the common law on the theory that the experience of buyers forewarned them that the sellers puffed their goods. The buyers were free to reject the intended reference or come to another conclusion.

Suppose A intends to defraud B when he contracts to sell him land or merchandise or securities. Even if there is insufficient evidence to prove fraud, if there is sufficient to prove that A has not performed his obligation, the law will enforce the contract or give damages "as if" he had intended to give good title or merchandise of the quality stipulated or the security promised. For the purpose of the case it will pretend that the intention and the understanding communicated mean one and the same thing.*

* It is not necessary for the purposes of this discussion to consider situations in which a court of equity would set aside a contract for fraud. Other special situations exist with respect to contracts, as, for example, some of those involved in the doctrine of equivocation.[13]

Legislation

A judicial function is to find the "intent" of framers of the Constitution or legislators, and it does so by "construing" the language in order to give effect to their intent. It is not possible for any legislative body to foresee all possible applications of law. Therefore, it is necessary for courts to weigh specific situations and determine whether they come within the legislative "intent," that is, what the legislators wished to accomplish, their expectations as to what situations the law would cover. Consequently the courts look to the evil to be remedied and first apply the ordinary meaning of words and any technical meanings of words which may be applicable. In other words, the judges apply their own experience and expectations to find the experience and expectations of legislators.[14]

The indefiniteness of legislation is illustrated by the Constitutional prohibition against impairment of the obligation of contracts. Courts have attempted to give definiteness to this clause by determining what is meant by a contract, by the obligation of a contract, by impairment and law. Courts are faced with the problem of how much weight to give to the expectations of the Constitution-makers or lawmakers at the time the Constitution or law was adopted and how much to the contemporary meaning of the words and their effect on contemporary conditions. "One judge, because of his training and experience, may have one view as to what are such fundamental principles and how they apply in a particular case, and an equally competent judge may have precisely opposite views. The same individual may have different views at different periods in his life as to what is 'permissible' and what is 'improper'!"[15]

Thus in interpretation or construction of legislation, the courts are clearly looking not for intent but intendment, "true meaning as fixed by law." *

In McBoyle v. United States, Mr. Justice Holmes said:

> Although it is not likely that a criminal will carefully consider the text of the law before he murders or steals, it is reasonable that a fair warning should be given to the world in language that the common world will understand, of what the law intends to do if a certain line is passed. To make the warning fair, so far as possible the line should be clear.[17]

This suggests that what is spoken by legislators and courts may not be the expectation that it will govern the conduct of "a criminal" or give him a choice of behavior, but that the common world of those who enforce the law may be clear as to their function. If the enforcers of the law are clear, then may not their consciences be clear in enforcing the law though such clarity is not apparent to the offender?

Dodd suggests that especially true, certainly with respect to the Constitutional law of the United States, is Bishop Hoadly's statement that "whoever hath an absolute authority to interpret any written or spoken laws, it is he who is truly the law-giver to all intents and purposes, and not the person who first wrote or spoke them." [18]

In conclusion, it might be noted that we are continually confusing *ought* and *reality*. "This mutual interaction between ought and reality is parallel to the interaction between want and reality." [19] Consequently a contracting party will see

* Morris R. Cohen comments that: "When in fact the president, a majority of the members of the House of Representatives, of the Senate, and a minority or perhaps even a majority of all the judges who have passed on the act, have expressed a contrary view, one would think that a sense of humor as well as of courtesy would prevent even a majority of a court from setting up their own opinions as the only rational one." [16]

what he wants the agreement to mean to be the reality of what it does mean. To him what he *wants ought* to be his engagement. What he *wants ought* to be the commitment of the opposite party. The judge in his turn, in interpreting a document, will perceive what he feels to be proper in the situation. His *ought* will emerge as the reality of the obligations assumed by the parties, the disposition contemplated by the testator, or the legislator's effort to remedy a situation. But this may be far from their "intent" or what they meant or expected or wished.

VII Conclusion

Law and Change

LAW IS at once the codification of experience into expectations of conduct and a declaration of the conditions under which the full coercive power of the State will if necessary be used to enforce these expectations.[1] Thus it establishes the norms which those holding prevailing sovereign powers will seek to enforce. In this connection, Herskovits quotes Hoebel, "A social norm is legal . . . if its neglect or infraction is met by the application, in threat or in fact, of the absolute coercive force by a social unit possessing the socially recognized privilege of so acting." [2] Consequently a finding of guilt or fault is a function of the court's perception of social expectation and experience. If there were no way of expressing and enforcing such expectations, society as a whole and individual members would lack stability. It is law that provides an instrument of the state to maintain the stability of the power of those who hold the prevailing instruments of sovereignty, stability by enforcement of their norms, and stability in the relationships between and among individuals and institutions relying on these norms. In other words, without law people would not know where they stood with respect to others and the government, what enforceable rights they had.

The need for this balance has been touched on (pp. 91, 169).

This does not mean that all who subscribe to the norms of law and have adapted their conduct to it like it, accept it as "good," or find that it meets their individual needs. However, observance of social norms is a defense against personal instability which occurs when one is socially dissident.

> And, since, my soul, we cannot fly
> To Saturn or to Mercury,
> Keep we must, if keep we can,
> These foreign laws of God and man.[3]

When people say that law tries to maintain the status quo, they are right; but, of course, as in any other field, this is not possible. Change is constantly occurring and the law must adapt to change if it is to fulfill its role of maintaining stability, of declaring those situations in which power would be exercised by the State in such a way as to maintain its stability effectively. Therefore, the law has had to adjust to social, political, and cultural changes.

Cardozo described the inconstancy of society and therefore the unavoidable inconstancy in law:

> The kinetic forces are too strong for us. We may think the law is the same if we refuse to change the formulas. The identity is verbal only. The formula has no longer the same correspondence with reality. Translated into conduct, it means something other than it did.[4]

One such important change was to adopt the concept of intentionality instead of relying on mere chance events to fix responsibility. The very adoption of the concept of intent as an element in crime and certain civil actions (and there was no clear line between them in early times) in itself tended to maintain stability because it avoided the dissonance or conflict between the old law, which based guilt or responsibility on the fact that the injury would not have occurred if the defendant had been nowhere in the chain of events, and the religious concept of free will which taught that people were endowed by their Creator with the capacity to choose between good and evil. In psychological terms, *intent* mediated between these two concepts.

The introduction of intent as an element of crimes was an ameliorating development. A man no longer need be convicted of a serious, hated offense for an occurrence that was accidental, casual, or unavoidable and then left to the uncertain remedy of an appeal to the Crown for clemency. This was an important reform in criminal justice.* But difficult as it has always been to "learn the secret thing contained in the heart of a man," may it not have been more readily learnable in a rural, homogeneous community of neighbors than in our twentieth-century urban society? May the guess, which at best a finding of intent must be, not have been more accurate several hundreds of years ago than it would be likely to be today?

Through the clumsy mechanisms of the law we attempt to distinguish the act done by the evil hand with an evil mind from other acts. We have changed our value system from one by which a man was held responsible for any results of his acts to one by which the degree of his responsibility or even any responsibility is mediated by his capacity to make a choice. But what is the capacity of any specific man—not generalized Man—to make a choice? This, as we have shown, is dependent

* Similarly, absolute liability for tortious acts was being modified and defenses were broadened.[5]

on, is a function of, his culture and subculture, the force of his unconscious and the power of his conscious control, and the influences bearing upon him.

Feedback

Essential to the maintenance of stability of any organism, whether physiological or social, is *feedback*. It is needed by legal institutions if their procedures and norms are to remain in balance with each other and with other institutions. The administrative and legislative branches of government, in order to maintain social balance, must get feedback from the courts and vice versa. Look, for example, at Brown v. The Board of Education, etc.,[6] where the Court held that segregation of children in the public schools, when based solely on their race, deprived children of minority groups of equal educational opportunities and therefore violated the Fourteenth Amendment.

Feedback of change in educational conditions and social conditions was slow to reach the Court, in spite of Mr. Dooley's dictum that the Supreme Court listens to the election returns, which means really looks for feedback from the prevailing view of the nation.

Chief Justice Warren said:

> In approaching this problem, we cannot turn the clock back to 1868 when the Amendment was adopted, or even to 1896, when *Plessy* v. *Ferguson* was written. We must consider public education in the light of its full development and its present place in American life throughout the Nation.[7]

In the Brown case, the Supreme Court did not consider the problem of de facto segregation in northern schools. In other words, it did not anticipate the problems that this raised or many other problems coming out of the Brown decision. On the other hand, the imbalance created by the decision was not promptly recognized by either state or federal administrative or legislative branches of government. Although generally more sensitive to feedback of a political nature than the courts, they were reluctant to act until civil rights demonstrations occurred in many parts of the country which gave to them tardy feedback that the law and the feelings of a large part of the nation were in disequilibrium. There is no well-developed system of feedback in the law. It is sluggish in registering change and imbalance and in anticipating trends.

This is apparent when one considers the legal history of slavery in the United States from the adoption of Article I, Section 3 of the Constitution to the Dred Scott decision and the Civil War, which resulted from inadequate feedback or recognition of the meaning of the feedback, and consequently incapacity to overcome resistance to the changes that were occurring. This is true in other fields of substantive law. The law was slow to recognize the changes brought about by industrialization, which required different ways of dealing with employers' liability. We know more about drug addicts and homosexuals, for example, than we did when the laws respecting them were written. Here social norms, embodied in the law, are too emotion-laden for most courts and legislators to accept feedback from the failure of legal attempts to solve such deviances or from what has been learned by psychiatry and medicine. Adjective law, that is legal procedures, are in open conflict with knowledge gained in other disciplines, especially social psychology.[8] Lawyers, like other people, tend to set up defensive mechanisms such as denial of realities that conflict with their own traditions, their legal systems of belief.

Change is not simply a matter of new law made by legislators and courts. These are a reflection of social, political, and economic changes to which law must accommodate to remain in balance with other phases of the national culture. In a scientific sense, law, political and social conditions, education and human needs are functions of each other, they interact to affect and modify one another. Although, as has been mentioned, substantive changes are often difficult, by comparison procedural and institutional changes may present even more serious difficulties. For they may involve changes in attitudes and skills of lawyers, and the relationships of law to other institutions and other disciplines. Here it is not only the law but lawyers and jurists who strive to maintain balance and reluctantly diverge from a presumed if illusory status quo. Change must consequently appear threatening to them, be itself unbalancing, and give rise to anxiety. Every change in a code of procedure may make useless skills and knowledge developed under the old.

We might apply Merton's schema of institutionalized goals and means (pp. 51–53). While as lawyers we may fully accept the institutionalized goals of the law, we need not accept the institutionalized means to legal goals.*

But when law fails to meet the current needs of society, when it no longer provides acceptable institutionalized means to achieve acceptable institutionalized goals, people disregard it or evade it or avoid it. If law fails to meet their needs for

* We must expect also that many lawyers who feel threatened by any questioning of institutionalized means will take such questioning to be a denial of the goals. In defense of their equilibrium they may distort the efforts of others to reform the means by equating this to an attack on goals and moral values of society. On another level this is the pattern traditionally used by counsel in trial to prejudice the court or jury against a party or witness because of some behavior which may even be irrelevant to the issues of the case. In other words, if a man behaves deviantly the inference is made that he thinks deviantly and the judgment follows that he's a "bad" man.

balance, it no longer commands their respect and support. Foster demonstrates this with reference to divorce law in New York (before its amendment in 1966).[9] Law no longer operates to provide norms which will be followed because they are felt to be desirable, that is, to meet needs. It may even establish norms for its evasion, as Foster shows. In such circumstances it does not operate as a successful instrument of sovereignty for it no longer contributes adequately to the maintenance of social stability.

Law not only sets norms for socially acceptable behavior but also its own rituals by which to determine deviance from those norms. It establishes procedures by which such deviances are to be handled in the interest of social stability within the state. But the norms and rituals of law, as has been indicated, may differ not only from one national culture to another, but may conflict with the norms acceptable to subcultures. Deviance from certain norms, as for example murder, theft, rape, incest, are punishable in all cultures. They may, however, be very differently defined and dealt with. Execution by the state is not defined as murder, whether it be execution of a single offender, of "war criminals" or slaughter by an atom bomb. Though definitions of "legitimate warfare" may differ, what has been said of primitive societies is apposite to us: "Attacks on human life outside the political unit are conceived of as legitimate warfare and entail no sanction save the diffuse, voluntary sanction of the revenge which chances of war might offer." [10] Larceny by shoplifting is a crime. But generally it is not a crime to give misleading information through advertising or merchandising though this may take money from people (especially poor people, who are less likely than others to have experienced judgment) by selling goods and services which are not equal to their representation or which, as in the case of cigarettes, may be dangerous to health and life. Communist doctrine forbids private enterprise because it assumes that it must inevitably result in exploitation of one person by another, the weaker by the stronger, the servant by the master, the buyer by the seller. This must be a crime under communist social norms. However, if a communist state through its government stores should sell shoddy merchandise to a consumer, and so exploit him, he is without remedy because he may not challenge an act of his government. Mention has already been made in Chapter II of the great cultural variations in definition of incest, under which the same relationship may be in one culture required for marriage and in another prohibited. Until recently, an Englishman was forbidden by law to marry his deceased wife's sister so that in order to avoid incestuous behavior, Max Beerbohm had to cross the Channel and marry his wife's sister on the Continent.

The United States has, as has often been stated, a pluralistic society. While generally not recognized at law, juries and probably judges at times have applied this concept. Thus where crimes of violence have been committted by Negroes against Negroes or by Indians against Indians, juries have sometimes been more lenient than if the offense had been committed by a white against a white because they have viewed "the defendant as not fully acculturated and therefore incapable of white standards of self-control." [11] (The feeling of whites against nonwhites in such situations has been previously discussed.)

While such a result may express contempt more than tolerance, Kalven and Zeisel suggest: "Conceivably, the law might recognize cultural differences and apply different norms to subcultures within the society, as indeed British colonialism appears to have done on occasion."[12]

Intent as an Issue of Fact or a Factor in Sentencing

Not only is it difficult to evaluate the freedom of choice and capacity of any individual to act on his choice because of (1) differences in value systems within the same culture (Chapter II), (2) differing degrees of conscious control over a broad continuum from spontaneous behavior to cognitive decision (Chapter III), and (3) the effects of drugs and possible imbalance of secretions in the blood stream (Chapter IV), but difficulties are implicit in judgment of another person's intent (Chapter V). Furthermore the controversial atmosphere of the courtroom makes anything close to a realistic evaluation of intent unlikely, if not impossible; adversary proceedings tend to produce victories rather than realities. Where intent is important as an element of litigation it could better be determined in other ways. It is a mental state even more difficult to determine than a physical condition. But unlike a physical condition intent must be deduced from a complex of sociopsychological interactions.

In spite of the limits of perception and recall which militate against reality in testimony, we have to utilize our present trial processes until, as the result of empirical research, lawyers can develop better methods of judging reality. To abandon them without replacing them with new trial procedures or substituting new institutional methods to handle litigation, criminal and civil, would leave a vacuum in legal process. It would create disequilibrium in government and imbalance in the lives of people.

However, the trial can be limited to determining whether P performed certain acts, whether behavior of his resulted in the injury for which he is prosecuted or sued for damages. But the question of *intent should properly be considered not as an element of the offense but as a factor to be determined and considered in specifying the treatment* to which he is to be subjected. Is he a person whose history indicates that he has been repeatedly unable to restrain his impulses so that he endangers others (or perhaps himself) or cannot refrain from destroying or stealing the property of others? This is not a problem of intent. It matters not whether he intended to injure others in their person or their property. The needs of society are that he be kept in custody or placed under observation or treatment.

The question of intent, however, becomes relevant in determining the kind of custody and the nature of the therapy to be given him. Is he perhaps a person who does not require custodial control but psychotherapy or special education? Here his intent is a factor in the determination of therapy, not in determining whether he has committed a wrongful act.*

* Leifer writes: "Since responsibility is *by definition* a function of intention, it logically follows that responsibility is definitionally related to the diagnosis of mental illness. . . .

"The court is charged with determining the responsibility of the defendant in two senses. First, it must determine whether the accused is *descriptively* responsible for the crime with which he is charged." In other words, did the accused, by his behavior, bring about the consequences which it is charged constitute a crime committed by him? "Second, the court must *ascribe* responsibility, that is to say, it must determine whether or not the defendant should be punished. . . . Descriptive and ascriptive responsibility are thus independent, and a man may be descriptively responsible in that it is proven that he did it, in fact kill Y, but responsibility may not be ascribed in that additional facts demonstrate the act to be an accident which could not have been prevented by more prudent action. . . . To put it another way, criminal responsibility is ascribed if (a) descriptive responsibility

In other words, the treatment or therapy to be given should be related to such questions as, Did he knowingly act with an evil hand and an evil mind? If he caused injury he should not be held to be without responsibility because he lacked intent—or because intent cannot be deduced from the evidence—any more than because he was stupid, incompetent, or reckless. Fromm has made this clear in another connection.

> We cannot understand *how* and *why* he became what he is, but we can also judge him as to *what* he is. . . . Assuming the shoes or the painting to be of poor quality, and that somebody pointed to the fact that the shoemaker or the painter had tried very hard but that certain conditions made it impossible for him to do better, I will not in either case change my judgment of the product. I may feel sympathy or pity for the shoemaker or the painter, I may feel tempted to help him, but I can not say that I can not judge his work because I understand why it is so poor. . . . Understanding a person does not mean condoning; it only means that one does not accuse him as if one were God or a judge placed above him.[14]

Suppose we were to divide the problem of guilt or liability when it is an element in litigation into two parts: First, did P do the particular act, i.e., behave in the manner charged, and was his behavior a proximate cause of the harm that was done? Second, was P's act, his behavior, the result of conscious intent, or was P serving an unconscious purpose and did he have a conscious choice on which he was capable of acting?

The first question deals with responsibility. Being held responsible for one's behavior is not only necessary to the social equilibrium, but is therapeutic for the individual involved, with the exception of those sociopaths who are incapable of avoidance learning, that is, learning from experience.

---

is proven and (b) it is not demonstrated that there are facts which indicate self-defense, accident, or mental illness." [13]

The principle of holding a person responsible for his behavior has a deep effect in shaping the personality and eventually results in making the person what he is. It has an influence on all who are brought up according to these principles. If a "wrong-doer" is made responsible for his act, all the members of his group will be influenced by this. . . .[15]

The second problem, however, is concerned with the personality of P and should be considered a basis for the disposition of the case, whether that be custodial or therapeutic treatment, or in a civil case, the award of punitive damages.

Inadequate as testimony may be because of the inaccuracy of our perception and recall, our processes of litigation may result in some semblance of reality when limited to externals. But the procedures of litigation are far too clumsy, too controversial, too punitive to answer on a basis of reality the second question—was the act one of conscious choice? *The finding of intent is a psychological finding. It is not a finding of a physical or physiological fact,* though the time may come when an analysis of blood chemistry, muscular tension, heartbeat, skin reaction, contraction of the pupil, or some other physical response may give us reliable clues to psychological states.

However, Pound points out, as a matter of fact "We know that the old analysis of act and intent can stand only as an artificial legal analysis and that the mental elements in crime present a series of difficult problems."

He is of course right. Study of the motivating traits and factors of criminalism shows how little, in most instances, there is of "free will." [16]

One who commits a crime or a tortious act in which intent is regarded to be an element probably may have less "free will," less freedom of choice in the particular situation than do others. For the violation of social norms in itself may be symptomatic of a lack of capacity to control need-drives and thus a weak ability to choose. This point was missed by the draftsmen of the *Model Penal Code*.[17]

A history of unconventional behavior, of deviance from social norms, may indicate "mental illness," and if the party were suffering from mental illness, this in itself would contradict the possibility of intention for it would be unlikely that he would have freedom of choice. Leifer says:

> *It is therefore a history of unconventional behavior of a socially disruptive nature which defeats the ascription of both mental health and intention.* The diagnosis of mental illness logically implies the absence of choice or intention because they are both defeated by the same kinds of facts.[18]

It is not suggested that all forms of unconventional behavior can be ascribed to mental illness. It is not necessarily true that deviance equals mental illness equals not guilty. As was stated in Chapter II, deviance may be a way to maintain mental health; or what is deviant to the prevailing culture may be appropriate to a subculture and therefore an expression of mental health.

In criminal cases, just as in cases involving tort liability, if one thinks primarily in terms of penalizing fault, one may bypass justice. Many times an accidental occurrence is attributed to someone's intent. (See pp. 74, 144, 148.) Many times an apparently accidental occurrence is caused intentionally, the intent or chain of action being concealed consciously or in the unconscious, in which case the actor himself may be unaware of it. Therefore, it makes little sense to treat crime and punishment from the point of view of intentional wrongdoing, for all too often the innocent will suffer and the guilty escape. Furthermore let us be aware that what we punish may not be the intended wrongful behavior of another person but an act which *we judge* to be wrongful in order to maintain our own sense of social balance. Our judgment may issue from a defense mechanism of our own, such as projection or identification. It necessarily will be based on our perceptions, founded on our own individual experience, which leads to our expectation that P must have done x. Such expectation may be in the form of some stereotype that says Ps probably do x whenever they get the chance. (Negroes will rape white women whenever they get the chance; whites will discriminate against Negroes whenever they get the chance; Armenians will sell you rugs and misrepresent them whenever they get the chance; etc.)

Even when we are not in a position to make a legal finding of guilt we tend to pass judgment, as Fromm points out.

> But many persons who have not the office of a judge assume the role of a judge, ready to condemn or absolve, when they make moral judgments. Their attitude often contains a good deal of sadism and destructiveness. There is perhaps no phenomenon which contains so much destructive feeling as "moral indignation," which permits envy or hate to be acted out under the guise of virtue. The "indignant" person has for once the satisfaction of despising and treating a creature as "inferior," coupled with the feeling of his own superiority and righteousness.[19]

Certainly, the mental elements that Pound referred to can be better defined by a study of wrongdoing by processes other than examination and cross-examination. There may be conflicting opinions or clues as to the mental elements in the case, primarily P's intention to do wrong, but such conflicts concerning the reality of his intention are not determinable by adversary proceedings, by so unscientific a procedure as the conflict of litigation. *We may now laugh at the belief that an issue of fact could be settled through ordeal by battle; but may it not be equally absurd to determine a state of mind, intention, by a courtroom battle, the contentiousness of litigation?* *

A psychological finding such as intent can be better determined by psychological tests and psychiatric examinations and from biographical data which can be more accurately obtained and more carefully considered by the court outside the trial procedures.[21] And certainly the lawyers should be present and free to question and discuss the data presented to the judge.

The suggestion here made is that the trial shall determine whether a wrongful act, an act contrary to law and injurious to another person, has been committed and that the mental processes of the defendant, his intention, shall be considered separately as data on which disposition of the case should be based. But what about a case of fraud or misrepresentation or forgery in which the intent to deceive is a basic element? In fraud cases it is the very intent to deceive that distinguishes them from cases of breach of contract or warranty. Perhaps what is really meant by intention in such cases is the *expectation* that another person will *believe* the statement or representation known by the defendant to be false or misleading and will *act* on it. Knowledge of falsity would be easier to

* It was the assumption that in an ordeal by battle Providence would give strength and skill to the righteous, so that virtue would be triumphant. Do we not assume, naïvely that innocence will shine forth and be perceived by judge and jury? We are reminded by Meredith that "the world is ever gracious to an hypocrisy that pays homage to the mask of virtue by copying it; the world is hostile to the face of an innocence not conventionally simpering and quite surprised; the world prefers decorum to honesty." [20]

prove than intent, which almost always must remain an inference.

In any event, in a fraud case it is difficult to see how the mental processes of the defendant could be eliminated from consideration of the triers of fact (jury or judge). But in determining sentence or judgment the judge can take into consideration not only the evidence of the trial but those subcultural and psychological factors relating to the defendant which may indicate the degree of his freedom of choice and therefore, of his intent. In a civil case for fraud such a proceeding is certainly relevant to the imposition of punitive damages and the judge's power to set them aside where the jury determines upon them.*

If intent is treated as an element in fixing sentence, determining damages, or recommending therapy, this is a process with which our courts have long been familiar. It would give the judge greater latitude to find the reality of intent than does a trial with or without a jury. And it would be a constitutional process. The leading case on the constitutionality of a modern sentencing procedure is Williams v. New York.[23] The question was whether the due process clause of the Fourteenth Amendment requires that one convicted of crime be permitted to confront and cross-examine witnesses as to his prior record or whether the sentencing judge may receive information about his previous record and consider it in sentencing. It was held that it did not violate the Constitution to permit the sentencing judge wide discretion as to the sources and types of

* While it is sometimes thought that malicious defamation involves intent this would not seem to be so in view of the decision of the Supreme Court in *New York Times Company v. Sullivan*.[22] A statement is then defined as made with actual malice when made "with knowledge that it was false or with reckless disregard of whether it was false or not."

information which he used in imposing sentence. Speaking for the majority of the Court, Mr. Justice Black stated:

> In addition to the historical basis for different evidentiary rules governing trial and sentencing procedures there are sound practical reasons for the distinction. In a trial before verdict the issue is whether a defendant is guilty of having engaged in certain criminal conduct of which he has been specifically accused. . . . A sentencing judge, however, is not confined to the narrow issue of guilt. His task within fixed statutory or constitutional limits is to determine the type and extent of punishment after the issue of guilt has been determined. Highly relevant—if not essential—to his selection of an appropriate sentence is the possession of the fullest information possible concerning the defendant's life and characteristics. (pp. 246, 247)

The Court considered that modern treatment of offenders made it necessary to distinguish between "the evidential procedure in the trial and sentencing processes." Mr. Justice Black said:

> In general, these modern changes have not resulted in making the lot of offenders harder. On the contrary a strong motivating force for the changes has been the belief that by careful study of the lives and personalities of convicted offenders many could be less severely punished and restored sooner to complete freedom and useful citizenship. (p. 249)

Finally, he said:

> We cannot say that the due process clause renders a sentence void merely because a judge gets additional out-of-court information to assist him in the exercise of this awesome power of imposing the death sentence. (p. 252)

In this connection, it should be noted that the Court had before it a publication of the Administrative Office of the United States Courts setting forth suggestions for probation reports which included an item on "Health (physical and mental)." *

It has also been held that where a jury determines punishment of a convicted defendant, nonlegal evidence may be presented to it to assist it in coming to a conclusion.[25]

Two recent cases, State v. Lucas (N.J.) and People v. Moseley (N.Y.), support such procedure.[26]

In his concurring opinion in Lucas, Weintraub, C.J., stated that he believed *M'Naughten* could not be abandoned. But he went on to say that society must be protected from the insane as well as the sane, and that the dispute is whether a criminal or civil process should be used. "If we could think of a conviction simply as a finding that the mortal in question has demonstrated his capacity for anti-social conduct, most of the battle would be decided. What would remain is the employment of such post-conviction techniques as would redeem the offender if he can be redeemed and secure him if he cannot." [27]

In accordance with this, Chief Justice Weintraub felt that in a capital case, in those jurisdictions in which the jury determines the penalty, a psychiatrist should be allowed to testify without being constrained by *M'Naughten* in order to allow the jury to decide whether the death penalty should be inflicted. This testimony would be relevant on the issue of punishment rather than guilt. In Moseley, Breitel, J., writing for the unanimous court, distinguished between "legal" insanity

* It has been held that it is not a violation of the Fifth Amendment to introduce at the trial the results of a physical examination, blood test, fingerprints, urinalysis, or handwriting even though obtained without the consent of the accused so long as these are procured without threat or violence.[24]

in determination of guilt under the "traditional and arguably archaic" M'Naughten rule and "medical" insanity which may be considered by the jury at the sentencing proceeding. Evidence "irrelevant at the main trial," such as the defendant's background, history and capacity to control his actions, would be relevant as a "mitigating circumstance" in fixing the penalty.

Punitive Character of Law

Uppermost in the law's approach to crime is the punitive aspect. This is true also in tort law. We speak, for example, of "punitive damages." By punishing the guilty we find release from our sense of guilt, we can project our own hostile impulses and deviances on others. If we felt that we had punished someone without justification, without being able to find that he was guilty, without an opportunity for projection and rationalizing about his guilt, we could not find release from our own punitive and hostile tensions. We would instead feel guilty. We are relieved of this guilt, as has been pointed out, by the concept of intent, by finding that the deed of which P has been accused was done by *his* evil hand with *his* evil mind. Moreover, if the person punished did not appear guilty, we could not cure him of his social deviance and change him, that is, remake him into a useful, law-abiding member of society. This would destroy a prop from under our sense of self-constancy, our image of ourselves as law-abiding people who protect society by enforcing its codes, who in justice and kindness try to redeem even as we punish.*

* Lasswell and Donnelly write, "One must not lose sight of the fact that an examination of a specific culture will show that it is characterized by permissive or even adulatory evaluations of cruelty in the name of punishment. There is no place for cruelty as an end in itself in a value system committed to human dignity." [28]

To a psychiatrist, however, punitive responses to behavior generally impede therapy. In other words, if we really believe that law should be used to reform offenders, we cannot say punish *and* reform. Furthermore, except when an offender desires and often invites punishment to justify and compensate for his guilt feelings, people who are found guilty are not likely to feel that society has treated them fairly. "Until a prisoner's bitterness over an unfair legal process has been overcome, the correctional process will not work." [29]

Law, symbolized by policeman and judge, is an ever-present threat of force, a punitive superego, even when not in consciousness. Consequently, to be arrested, summoned before a grand jury, or tried in court is in itself a punishing experience which reduces one's sense of social power.[30] But, of course, the extent to which it is felt to be punishing (and whether the punishment is sought by the offender or not) and reduces his sense of social power is a function of each individual's personality, his ego-defense, and experience. We can assume that even when without punitiveness one is held accountable for his deviant behavior he will nevertheless feel punished, that the accounting itself is punitive, if he is a normal, not a sociopathic, individual.

We have seen in Chapter III how hostility arises as the result of a sense of reduction of social power. What could give one a greater reduction of a sense of social power than conviction after a trial in which one is charged with crime and then committed to a prison—or a mental institution. Of course, in many cases, too, the offense itself is committed as an act of hostility arising out of a sense of lack or loss of social power and a feeling that the world is against one.

Indications are that therapy, not punishment, should be the aim of correction. If therapy is today not practicable, as in the case of some repeated offenders (such as many compulsive neurotics and sociopaths and participants in the crimes of the Nazi Party and regime) or certain kinds of mental illness, then there should be detention, for the protection of the wrongdoer or society or both. Here a caveat is in order. The history of the administration of prisons, workhouses, and mental institutions and many Poor Laws shows that they have been used to get the dirty villains off the streets, to put them away where they cannot infect others with their sinfulness (to the Puritan conscience which we in part inherit, poverty can be sinful), and keep such unsolved problems as crime, poverty, and mental illness out of our consciousness.

It is extremely difficult to make therapy the aim of our corrective institutions as they are now set up. Among other things, there are generally not adequate facilities for therapy. But more important, our attitude toward offenders and the attitudes of present personnel generally call for punishment. The punitive system of the law, as has been indicated, answers certain needs to unleash hostility on the part of individuals and the community. Moreover, the personnel of prisons and mental institutions, though in theory committed to therapeutic treatment of the inmates, frequently see their roles as punitive and act out their own hostile drives on people who cannot successfully retaliate.

This is not the place to discuss at length the problems of penology except insofar as there is interconnection between hostility of the law toward deviants and hostility by personnel of prisons and mental institutions toward them. Punitive people in our society and punitive courts demand and expect punitive treatment of prisoners and patients. This in turn encourages punitiveness by institutional personnel and reinforces such attitudes by the public (including the press) and the courts. Hospitals, too, can for the inmates be prisons in fact. As the superintendent of Galesburg State Research Hospital in Illinois wrote:

> It is important to recognize also that commitment can be a form of incarceration, and prosecutors, judges and hospital officials are not immune to this expectation of society. . . . Often this is quite anti-therapeutic, but prejudice prevails over reason, and individual "civil rights" are conveniently overlooked.[31]

However difficult it is not to be hostile when faced with a horrifying crime, we have to recognize that punishment, because of the defense mechanisms it stimulates in an offender, is contradictory to attempts to bring about positive personality changes. As Stagner indicates:

> By and large, learning data indicate that reward is more effective than punishment. It is particularly clear that prolonged punishment has repercussions of great strength. The educational data on the effects of repeated scolding and criticism, and level of aspiration studies on effects of continued failure are relevant here. . . . If there is anything to be learned from modern work in penology, it is that criminals are not reformed when vengeful and vindictive "justice" is meted out.[32]

Scientific Criteria for the Law

There has been so little basic change in Anglo-American law in recent centuries that we may forget that in England great changes occurred over the medieval centuries, beginning about the thirteenth. The law of the Year Books was by no means static. Anglo-Saxon origins, Canon law, Roman law, and the law merchant were affecting the development of the common law. Substantive and adjective law of the king's court were engaged in meeting competition from the other systems. The history of the law merchant is especially relevant.[33] Based on good faith more than formal documents, supported by Church morality, its roots reaching to the *realities of business enterprise,* the system of the law merchant threatened, in the mercantile field, the supremacy of the common law until the king's court absorbed it. Today our courts are in competition with arbitration systems and the judicial functions of administrative bodies, as well as threatened by dissatisfaction with the unrealities, the *As If* formulas, of the law which conflict with the findings of the social sciences.

In its development the common law created new writs to make possible the assertion of new substantive rights. If we conceive of the individual's treatment as *a* man rather than as *man* to be a right, then the law is challenged today to make such procedural modification as will protect that right. Should not the law make possible the treatment of John Doe the individual, not simply John Doe the hypothesized reasonable man with freedom to choose between good and evil?

There is, of course, much more to be learned about freedom of choice and intent than has been discovered, far more than has been set forth within this book. As the advancement of this knowledge is important to the development of law, it would seem desirable that lawyers participate in research concerning free choice and intent and the applications of the findings of such research to the problems of law. In such a process the social science disciplines could assist in giving to lawyers and jurists feedback. They could offer methods of reality testing which could help the adaptation of the law to social change and shorten the gap which always exists between law as it functions in an objective reality world and how its practitioners perceive it. The slow, centuries-long adaptation to change in the Middle Ages can be shortened in our time by the application of scientific inquiry.

It matters little whether this discussion of intent is accepted. It would be far better if it were challenged, not on the basis of authority, but by proposing questions to the solution of which scientific method might be applied.

The machines that scientists invent and technicians man can give us answers to many complex questions. But it remains for someone—scientist or legal scholar—to frame the questions so that significant answers can be obtained. Before problems of any kind can be solved they must first be stated. "Before helpful answers can be got, suitable questions must be asked." [34] Where legal problems are concerned, lawyers must be involved in framing the questions to which empirical answers are sought.

Most legal research is a compilation of authorities rather than the testing of hypotheses, that is, trying empirically to answer questions. The difference is well stated by Bernard in his classic, *An Introduction to the Study of Experimental Medicine:*

> The revolution which the experimental method has effected in the sciences is this: it has put a scientific criterion in the place of personal authority.
>
> The experimental method is characterized by being dependent only on itself, because it includes within itself its criterion—experience. It recognizes no authority other than that of facts and is free from personal authority.[35]

It would be difficult for courts to experiment. Questions of constitutionality might well arise and the purpose of law to contribute to the maintenance of social equilibrium might be threatened. The challenge is in the first instance to law schools working with psychologists and sociologists, with the interested participation of the judiciary, to engage in a program of reality testing. Perhaps the *As If* assumptions of the law are the best practical approaches to reality. Some of them undoubtedly will prove to be pragmatically valid. If so, well and good. But let us not accept them on authority or faith, or lethargically, or fearful of the changes that empirical evidence might imply.

Notes

INTRODUCTION

1. *Morisette v. United States*, 342 U.S. 246 (1951), p. 264.
2. See Rudolf Von Ihering, *Law as a Means to an End* (Boston: The Boston Book Company, 1913), p. xxiii.
3. *Morissette v. United States*, p. 252.
4. Hadley Cantril, "Sentio, Ergo Sum: 'Motivation' Reconsidered," *Journal of Psychology*, Vol. 65, 1967, p. 91.
5. *The Concise Oxford Dictionary of Current English*, 5th ed. (New York: Oxford University Press, 1964).
6. James A. H. Murray, ed. *A New English Dictionary on Historical Principles* (London: Oxford University Press, 1888–1928). [emphasis added]
7. See also *Encyclopaedia Britannica*, 1948 ed. Vol. 12 (Chicago), p. 463.
8. *Black's Law Dictionary*, 3rd ed. (St. Paul, Minn.: West Publishing Company, 1933), p. 48.
9. *Bouvier's Law Dictionary, a Concise Encyclopedia of the Law*, Rawle's Third Revision, Vol. II (St. Paul, Minn.: West Publishing Company, 1914).
10. *Black's Law Dictionary*, p. 993.

11. See *Proposed Official Draft of Model Penal Code*, American Law Institute, 1962, §210.2(1)(b).
12. *Corpus Juris Secundum*, 4 A (Brooklyn: American Law Book Company, 1946), pp. 11, 3 *et. seq.*
13. John Henry Wigmore, *A Treatise on the Anglo-American System of Evidence in Trial at Common Law*, Vol. I, 2nd ed. (Boston: Little, Brown and Company, 1923), §300.
14. Ralph Gerard, "Neurophysiology: An Integration," in *Handbook of Physiology*, H. W. Magoun, ed., Vol. 3 (Washington, D.C.: American Physiological Society, 1960), p. 1952; quoted in Cantril, p. 97.
15. *Ibid.*
16. Abraham J. Heschel, *God in Search of Man—a Philosophy of Judaism* (Philadelphia: Jewish Publication Society, 1955), pp. 295, 296, 314.
17. *Regina v. Charlson*, All English Law Reports (1955), 1, 859–864; 39 Criminal Appeals Reports (1955).
18. *Ibid.*, p. 860.
19. *Ibid.*, p. 860.
20. Oliver Wendell Holmes, Jr., *The Common Law* (Boston: Little, Brown and Company, 1881), p. 52.
21. *Ibid.*, p. 53.
22. Mr. Justice Jackson, in *Morissette v. United States*, pp. 251–252.
23. Max Radin, "Intent, Criminal," *Encyclopaedia of the Social Sciences*, Vol. 8 (New York: The Macmillan Company, 1937), p. 130.
24. *Ibid.*
25. Francis B. Sayre, "Public Welfare Offenses," *Columbia Law Review*, Vol. 33, 1933, p. 56.
26. See *Morissette v. United States*, pp. 251, 253–255, 270, and Gerhard O. W. Mueller, "Mens Rea and the Law Without It: Rationale and the West Virginia Rule," *West Virginia Law Review*, Vol. 58, 1955, pp. 34–68.

CHAPTER I

1. *Morissette v. United States*, 342 U.S. 246 (1951), p. 250.
2. N. M. Korkunov, *General Theory of Law*, trans. by W. G. Hastings (Boston: The Boston Book Company, 1909), p. 59.

3. Frederick Pollock and Frederic William Maitland, *The History of English Law*, Vol. II (Cambridge: Cambridge University Press, 1911), pp. 474–475.
4. W. S. Holdsworth, *A History of English Law*, Vol. V (Boston: Little, Brown and Company, 1924), fn. p. 417.
5. Pollock and Maitland, p. 475.
6. *Ibid.*, pp. 474–476.
7. *Ibid.*, p. 472.
8. *Ibid.*, fn. p. 476.
9. Pollock and Maitland, pp. 470–471. Compare Gerhard O. W. Mueller, "Tort, Crime and the Primitive," *Journal of Criminal Law, Crime and Police Science*, Vol. 46, 1955, pp. 303, 332.
10. Abraham J. Heschel, *God in Search of Man—a Philosophy of Judaism* (Philadelphia: Jewish Publication Society, 1955), p. 296.
11. Holdsworth, pp. 416, 417.
12. Karl Olivecrona, *Law as Fact* (London: Humphrey Milford, 1939), pp. 112–113.
13. Pollock and Maitland, pp. 598–600.
14. *Ibid.*, p. 474.
15. James George Frazer, *The Golden Bough—A Study in Magic and Religion*, abr. ed. (New York: The Macmillan Company, 1923), pp. 680–681.
16. E. Adamson Hoebel, *The Law of Primitive Man* (Cambridge, Mass.: Harvard University Press, 1954), p. 236.
17. J. P. Gillin, "Crime & Punishment Among the Barama River Carib," *American Anthropologist*, Vol. 36, pp. 331–344 at 335 (1934), quoted by Hoebel, p. 299.
18. Hoebel, p. 236.
19. Charles Howard McIlwain, *The Growth of Political Thought in the West* (New York: The Macmillan Company, 1932), p. 111.
20. *Ibid.*, p. 326.
21. *Ibid.*, pp. 191, 328, 330.
22. Pollock and Maitland, Vol. I, pp. 111, 124.
23. *Ibid.*, p. 129.
24. *Ibid.*, p. 130.
25. *Ibid.*, p. 128.
26. *Ibid.*, Vol. II, p. 465.
27. *Ibid.*, pp. 465–466.
28. *Ibid.*, p. 470.

29. Gerhard O. W. Mueller, "Mens Rea and the Law Without It: Rationale and the West Virginia Rule," *West Virginia Law Review*, Vol. 58, 1955; *Morissette v. United States*, pp. 251 fn., 252–258.
30. Deuteronomy 30:15–19, *The Holy Scriptures According to the Masoretic Text* (Philadelphia: The Jewish Publication Society of America, 1955), p. 278.
31. *The Nicomachean Ethics of Aristotle*, J. E. C. Welldon, trans., (London: Macmillan and Co., 1934) Book III, Chapters 5–7, pp. 69–76.
32. *Encyclopaedia Britannica*, 1948 ed. (Chicago), Vol. 9, p. 749.
33. Oliver Wendell Holmes, Jr., *The Common Law* (Boston: Little, Brown and Company, 1881), p. 55.
34. Melville J. Herskovits, *Man and His Works* (New York: Alfred A. Knopf, 1948) pp. 77–78.
35. See Leon Festinger, *A Theory of Cognitive Dissonance* (Evanston, Ill.: Row, Peterson and Company, 1957), and Jack W. Brehm and Arthur R. Cohen, *Explorations in Cognitive Dissonance* (New York: John Wiley and Sons, 1962), p. 106, where the authors distinguish between "dissonance processes" which "are either-or phenomenon" and "judgmental processes" which "admit of compromise."
36. Konrad Lorenz, *On Aggression* (New York: Harcourt, Brace and World, 1966), p. 231.
37. Hadley Cantril and Charles H. Bumstead, *Reflections on the Human Venture* (New York: New York University Press, 1960), p. 157.
38. Holmes, p. 213.
39. David Krech and Richard S. Crutchfield, *Elements of Psychology* (New York: Alfred A. Knopf, 1958), p. 222.
40. *Ibid.*, p. 223.

CHAPTER II

1. Karl Menninger and Joseph Statten, "What Psychiatry Proposes for Offenders," *Menninger Quarterly*, Vol. 15, No. 3, Fall, 1961, pp. 1–10.
2. James Marshall, "Evidence, Psychology, and the Trial: Some Challenges to Law," *Columbia Law Review*, Vol. 63, p. 197, Feb.

1963, and *Law and Psychology in Conflict* (Indianapolis: Bobbs-Merrill, 1966).

3. Sheldon Glueck, *Laws and Psychiatry, Cold War or Entente Cordiale?* (Baltimore: The Johns Hopkins University Press, 1962), p. 12.
4. Frederick Pollock and Frederic William Maitland, *The History of English Law*, Vol. II (Cambridge: Cambridge University Press, 1911), pp. 470–471.
5. Glueck, pp. 11, 12.
6. Fred L. Strodtbeck, Rita M. James, and Charles Hawkins, "Social Status in Jury Deliberations," *American Sociological Review*, Vol. 22, No. 6 (Dec. 1957), pp. 713–719.
7. Kurt Lewin, *Resolving Social Conflict* (New York: Harper & Row, Publishers, 1948), pp. 5–6.
8. *Ibid.*
9. *Ibid.*, p. 104; and see also Morton Deutsch, "Field Theory in Social Psychology," in *Handbook of Social Psychology*, Gardner Lindzey, ed. (Cambridge, Mass.: Addison-Wesley, 1954), p. 189.
10. *Ibid.*, p. 105.
11. C. C. North, *Social Differentiation* (Chapel Hill: University of North Carolina Press, 1927), p. 247.
12. John Adams, "Discourses on Davila," in *Works*, VI (Boston: Little, Brown and Company, 1851), pp. 239–240.
13. Katherine Mansfield, "Miss Brill," in *The Garden Party and Other Stories* (New York: Alfred A. Knopf, 1923).
14. T. Dembo, G. L. Leviton, and B. A. Wright, "Adjustment to Misfortune—a Problem of Social-Psychological Rehabilitation," *Artificial Limbs*, Vol. 3, No. 2, 1956, p. 22, cited by Fritz Heider, in *The Psychology of Interpersonal Relations* (New York: John Wiley and Sons, 1958), p. 96. The relativity of perceptions of the same person is illustrated in Lenore G. Marshall, *Hall of Mirrors* (New York: The Macmillan Company, 1937).
15. Hilda T. Himmelweit, "Socio-economic Background and Personality," in *Current Perspectives in Social Psychology*, E. P. Hollander and Raymond G. Hunt, eds. (New York: Oxford University Press, 1963), p. 134. See also the discussion of "inner-directed" and "other-directed" persons in American culture in David Riesman, *et al.*, *The Lonely Crowd* (Garden City, New York: Anchor Books, 1953); and discussion of "Child Training by Entrepreneurial and Bureaucratic Families," and different effects of

physical and other forms of punishment in *The Changing American Parent,* David R. Miller and Guy E. Swanson, eds. (New York: John Wiley and Sons, 1958).

16. Tamotsu Shibutani, "Reference Groups as Perspectives," in Hollander and Hunt, pp. 99, 100.
17. Joachim Israel, "The Effect of Positive and Negative Self-Evaluation in the Attractiveness of a Goal," *Human Relations,* Vol. 13, No. 1, 1960, pp. 33, 37.
18. Shibutani, p. 99.
19. Richard Hammer, "Report from a Spanish Harlem 'Fortress,'" *The New York Times Magazine,* January 5, 1964, pp. 22, 32, 37.
20. Isidor Chein, "Environment and Personality in Behavior Deviation," *19th Annual Meeting, New York Society of Clinical Psychologists,* 1967, p. 1.
21. *Ibid.*
22. James B. Conant, *The Education of American Teachers* (New York: McGraw-Hill Book Company, 1963), p. 115.
23. Shibutani, p. 105.
24. For an account of the relation between the effects of life in the Negro slum of Harlem and readiness to learn what schools offer, see Nat Hentoff, "Profiles," *The New Yorker,* May 7, 1966, pp. 70, 103, 109–110, 119.
25. Barbara A. McKinnon, "Educating Kids in the Ghetto: A Negro Teacher's Criticism," *New York World-Telegram and Sun,* school page, Nov. 17, 1965.
26. Leslie A. Fiedler, "The New Mutants," *Partisan Review* (Fall 1965), pp. 505, 514–515.
27. Hammer, p. 37. See also Gertrude Samuels, "I Don't Think the Cop Is My Friend," *The New York Times Magazine,* March 29, 1964, p. 28.
28. William P. Brown, "The Review Board Proposals Do Not Go Far Enough," Address at the 71st National Conference on Government, Nov. 17, 1965.
29. Herbert H. Hyman, "The Value Systems of Different Classes: A Social Psychological Contribution to the Analysis of Stratification," in *Class, Status and Power: A Reader in Social Stratification,* Richard Bendix and Seymour Martin Lipset, eds. (Glencoe, Ill.: The Free Press, 1953), p. 426.
30. *Industry and Society,* William Foote Whyte, ed. (New York: McGraw-Hill Book Company, 1946), p. 308; Alfred C. Kinsey

et al., "Social Level and Sexual Outlet," in Bendix and Lipset, p. 300.

31. Chein, pp. 11–13.
32. Hyman, pp. 426, 427; Robert Coles, "The Poor Don't Want to Be Middle Class," in *The New York Times Magazine*, Dec. 19, 1965, p. 7.
33. See Kenneth F. Walker, "Executives' and Union Leaders' Perceptions of Each Other's Attitudes to Industrial Relations: The Influence of Stereotypes," *Human Relations*, Vol. 15, No. 3, 1962, pp. 183, 193.
34. Maxim Gorky, "The Twenty-Six and One," in *Tellers of Tales*, W. Somerset Maugham, ed. (New York: Doubleday and Company, 1939), p. 647.
35. Allison Davis, "The Motivation of the Underprivileged Worker," pp. 84–106, in Whyte.
36. Herman Melville, *Billy Budd and the Piazza Tales* (New York: Dolphin Books, 1961).
37. Howard S. Becker, *Outsiders: Studies in the Sociology of Deviance* (Glencoe, Ill.: The Free Press, 1963), p. 9.
38. Gunnar Myrdal, *Challenge to Affluence* (New York: Pantheon Books, 1962), p. 51.
39. Raymond G. McCarthy, "Alcoholism: Attitudes and Attacks, 1775–1935," in *Understanding Alcoholism, The Annals, American Academy of Political and Social Science*, Vol. 315, Jan. 1958, pp. 16–17.
40. Jackson Toby, "Criminal Motivation," *British Journal of Criminology*, Vol. 2, No. 4, 1962, p. 317.
41. Hans H. Toch, "Psychological Consequences of the Police Role," presented at symposium at Annual Meeting of American Psychological Association, September 1, 1963.
42. *Gideon v. Wainwright*, 372 U.S. 335 (1963), overruling *Betts v. Brady*, 316 U.S. 455 (1942). See also *Douglas v. California*, 372 U.S. 353 (1963); *White v. Maryland*, 373 U.S. 59 (1963).
43. E. H. Sutherland, *White-Collar Crime* (New York: Holt, Rinehart and Winston, 1949); D. E. Cressy, "The Differential Association Theory and Compulsive Crimes," *Journal of Criminal Law, Criminology, and Police Science*, Vol. 45, 1954, pp. 35–38.
44. Henry H. Foster, Jr., "Divorce Reform," *Bar Bulletin*, New York County Lawyers Association, N.Y., Vol. 4, No. 22, 1964–1965, pp. 165, 168.

45. Jerome E. Carlin, Jan Howard, and Sheldon L. Messinger, "Civil Justice and the Poor: Issues for Sociological Research," *Law and Society Review*, Vol. 1, No. 1, Nov. 1966, pp. 10–14.
46. *Ibid.*, pp. 31–32.
47. See J. Robert Moskin, "Have Bigness, the Bomb and the Buck Destroyed Our Old Morality?" *Look*, Sept. 24, 1963, p. 75.
48. *U.S. v. Masonite Corporation*, 316 U.S. 265 (1942). See also *U.S. v. Patten*, 226 U.S. 525 (1913); *U.S. v. Reading Company*, 226 U.S. 324 (1912).
49. *U.S. v. General Electric Company*, Eastern District of Pa., No. 20236, Judgment filed 2/13/61. See also *The New York Times*, Feb. 7, 1961, p. 26, col. 5; Feb. 8, 1961, p. 16, col. 5.
50. Hannah Arendt, *On Revolution* (New York: The Viking Press, 1963), p. 102.
51. James Baldwin, *The Fire Next Time* (New York: The Dial Press, 1963), pp. 33, 108–109, 115; Yehudi A. Cohen, "Some Aspects of Ritualized Behavior in Interpersonal Relations," *Human Relations*, Vol. 11, No. 3, 1958, p. 196.
52. Riesman, p. 94.
53. Konrad Lorenz, *On Aggression* (New York: Harcourt Brace & World, 1966), pp. 169–171.
54. S. I. Hayakawa, "Meaning, Symbols and Levels of Abstraction," in *Readings in Social Psychology*, T. M. Newcomb and E. L. Hartley, eds. (New York: Henry Holt and Co., 1947), pp. 190–203.
55. Heider, p. 92.
56. Donald R. Matthews and James W. Prothro, "Southern Racial Attitudes: Conflict, Awareness, and Political Change," *The Annals, American Academy of Political and Social Science*, Vol. 344, 1962, pp. 108–121.
57. *Ibid.*, p. 111.
58. *Ibid.*, pp. 110, 111, 113. [emphasis added]
59. See Arthur R. Cohen, "Upward Communication in Experimentally Created Hierarchies," *Human Relations*, Vol. 11, No. 1, 1958, pp. 41–53; see also Rensis Likert, *New Patterns of Management* (New York: McGraw-Hill Book Co., 1961), pp. 46–55.
60. Toby, pp. 320–324.
61. Robert K. Merton, *Social Theory and Social Structure*, rev. and enl. ed. (Glencoe, Ill.: The Free Press, 1957), pp. 131–194.
62. *Ibid.*, pp. 132–134.

63. *Ibid.*, p. 140.
64. Joseph D. Lohman, "The Participant Observer in Community Studies," *American Sociological Review*, Vol. 2, 1937, pp. 890–898.
65. Kinsey, *et al.*, in Bendix and Lipset, p. 300.
66. Merton, p. 429.
67. Herskovits, pp. 77–78; see also pp. 461, 485–486.
68. *Ibid.*, pp. 66, 296–303.
69. "The Comanche" (compiled from information supplied by Ralph Linton) in *The Psychological Frontiers of Society*, Abraham Kardiner and associates, eds. (New York: Columbia University Press, 1945), pp. 47–80.
70. See discussion of "inner-directed" and "other-directed" persons in American culture, in Riesman, and discussion of "Child Training by Entrepreneurial and Bureaucratic Families," in Miller and Swanson, pp. 90–119.
71. Riesman, p. 74.
72. Toby, pp. 324, 325; Martin Gold, *Status Forces in Delinquent Boys* (Ann Arbor, Mich.: Institute for Social Research, 1963).
73. Toby, p. 324.
74. Merton, p. 158.
75. Leo Scrole, *et al.*, "Mental Health in the Metropolis," *The Midtown Manhattan Study*, Vol. 1 (New York: The McGraw-Hill Book Company, 1962).
76. *Ibid.*, p. 217.
77. K. Dalton, "Menstruation and Crime," *British Medical Journal*, No. 5269, December 30, 1961, pp. 1752–1753, Graph 1, Table 3.
78. See Leon Festinger, *A Theory of Cognitive Dissonance* (Evanston, Ill.: Row Peterson and Company, 1957), p. 264.
79. Gold, note 72.
80. Gordon W. Allport, *Personality and Social Encounter* (Boston: The Beacon Press, 1960), p. 77.
81. Edward A. Shils, "The Study of the Primary Group," in *The Policy Sciences*, Daniel Lerner and Harold D. Lasswell, eds. (Stanford: Stanford University Press, 1951).
81. Morton Deutsch, "The Interpretation of Praise and Criticism as a Function of Their Social Context," *Journal of Abnormal and Social Psychology*, Vol. 62, No. 2, 1961, pp. 391–400.
83. Ralph M. Stogdill, *Individual Behavior and Group Achievement* (New York: Oxford University Press, 1959), p. 170.

84. A. W. Clark and P. Van Sommers, "Contradictory Demands in Family Relations and Adjustment to School and Home," *Human Relations*, Vol. 14, No. 2, 1961, pp. 97–110.
85. *Ibid.*, p. 109.
86. Alberta Engvall Siegel and Sidney Siegel, "Reference Groups, Membership Groups and Attitude Change," in *Group Dynamics, Research and Theory*, Dorwin Cartwright and Alvin Zander, eds., 2nd ed. (Evanston, Ill.: Row, Peterson and Company, 1960), pp. 232–240; S. E. Asch, "Effects of Group Pressure upon the Modification and Distortion of Judgments," in Cartwright and Zander, pp. 189–200.
87. Muzafer Sherif, *The Psychology of Social Norms* (New York: Harper & Row, Publishers, 1936), p. 111.
88. Lefkowitz, *et al.*, "Status Factors in Pedestrian Violation of Traffic Signals," cited by Robert R. Blake and Jane Srygley Mouton, "Present and Future Implications of Social Psychology for Law and Lawyers," *Journal of Public Law*, Emory University Law School, Vol. 3, 1954, p. 356.
89. *Ibid.*, p. 357.
90. Arthur R. Cohen, p. 41.
91. Oscar Lewis, *Five Families* (New York: John Wiley and Sons, Science Editions, 1962), pp. 2–3. See also Matthews and Prothro.
92. Arthur R. Cohen, note 59.
93. Himmelweit, p. 31 *supra.*
94. Arthur R. Cohen, p. 52.
95. Murray Horwitz, David C. Glass, Seymour Giniger, and Alfred Cohn, "The Effect of Frustrating Acts Upon the Expectation of Openness," *Human Relations*, Vol. 19, No. 2, May 1966, p. 179.
96. Lewis, p. 2; and see introduction to Oscar Lewis, *La Vide* (New York: Random House, 1965), pp. xlii–lii.
97. Peter Blau, *The Dynamics of Bureaucracy* (Chicago: University of Chicago Press, 1955), p. 109.
98. *Ibid.*, pp. 99–116.
99. See Melville.
100. Edward Kasner and James Newman, *Mathematics and the Imagination* (New York: Simon and Schuster, 1940), p. 254.

CHAPTER III

1. Benjamin Cardozo, *The Nature of the Judicial Process* (New Haven: Yale University Press, 1921), p. 174.
2. Jacques Maritain, *Creative Intuition in Art and Poetry* (New York: Pantheon Books, 1953), pp. 94–95; and see Pope Pius XII, Address to the Congress of the International Association of Applied Psychology, April 10, 1958, cited by Oscar M. Ruebhausen and Orville G. Brim, Jr., "Privacy and Behavioral Research," *Columbia Law Review*, Vol. 65, No. 7, p. 1187.
3. See C. H. Waddington, *The Nature of Life* (New York: Atheneum, 1962), pp. 121–123.
4. Franz Alexander and Hugo Staub, *The Criminal, the Judge and the Public, a Psychological Analysis*, rev. ed. (New York: Collier Books, 1962), p. 97.
5. Maritain, p. 94.
6. W. A. Tillman and G. E. Hobbs, "The Accident-Prone Automobile Driver, a Study of the Psychiatric and Social Background," *American Journal of Psychiatry*, Vol. 106, 1949, p. 321; Fred J. Cook, "What Makes a Safe Driver Safe?" *The New York Times Magazine*, April 7, 1963, pp. 79–87; Ross A. McFarland, "Psychological and Psychiatric Aspects of Highway Safety," *Journal of the American Medical Association*, Vol. 163, 1967, p. 235.
7. *Regina v. Charlson*, All English Law Reports (1955), 1, 859–864; see also *Rex v. Harrison-Owen*, All English Law Reports (1951), 2, 726.
8. Alexander and Staub, p. 45.
9. Barbara W. Tuchman, *The Guns of August* (New York: The Macmillan Company, 1962), p. 316.
10. Irving Sarnoff, "Psychoanalytic Theory and Social Attitudes," *The Public Opinion Quarterly*, Vol. 24, 1960, p. 272.
11. Tuchman, p. 317.
12. Sarnoff, p. 256.
13. Gordon W. Allport, "The Open System in Personality Theory," in E. P. Hollander and Raymond G. Hunt, *Current Perspectives in Social Psychology* (New York: Oxford University Press, 1963), pp. 151, 155.
14. Sarnoff, p. 255.
15. Alexander and Staub, p. 99.

16. Alexander and Staub, p. 149.
17. See note 6, *supra.*
18. Irving Sarnoff, *Personality, Dynamics and Development* (New York: John Wiley and Sons, 1962), p. 354.
19. Alexander and Staub, p. 97.
20. Lawrence S. Kubie, "The Concept of Normality and Neurosis," in *Psychoanalysis and Social Work*, Marcel Heiman, ed. (New York: International Universities Press, 1953), pp. 3, 9; and Charles E. Osgood, "On the Nature of Meaning," in Hollander and Hunt, pp. 233, 235, 236.
21. Fedor Dostoevsky, *The Short Novels of Dostoevsky* (New York: The Dial Press, 1945), p. 129.
22. Alexander and Staub, p. 99.
23. Lawrence S. Kubie, "Social Forces and the Neurotic Processes," *Journal of Nervous and Mental Diseases*, Vol. 128, 1959, pp. 65, 67.
24. Lawrence S. Kubie, "Implications for Legal Procedure of the Fallibility of Human Memory," *Pennsylvania Law Review*, Vol. 108, 1959, pp. 59, 66, 68.
25. *The Basic Writings of Sigmund Freud*, A. A. Brill, ed. (New York: The Modern Library, 1938), p. 162. And see Theodor W. Adorno *et al.*, *The Authoritarian Personality* (New York: Harper and Brothers, 1950), pp. 457, 458.
26. Alexander and Staub, p. 97.
27. See Jonas Langner, Seymour Wapner, and Heinz Werner, "The Effect of Danger Upon the Experience of Time, *American Journal of Psychology*, Vol. 74, 1961, pp. 94, 97; see D. G. Doehring, "Accuracy and Consistency of Time-Estimation by Four Methods of Reproduction," *American Journal of Psychology*, Vol. 74, 1961, p. 27 (describing experiments on individuals' ability to judge time).
28. Gardner Murphy, *Personality* (New York: Harper & Row, Publishers, 1947), pp. 276–277.
29. Norman R. F. Maier, Nathan M. Glaser, and James B. Klee, "Studies of Abnormal Behavior in that Rat: III, The Development of Behavior Fixations Through Frustration," *Journal of Experimental Psychology*, Vol. 26, 1940, pp. 521–546.
30. Robert K. Merton, "The Self-Fulfilling Prophecy," in *Social Theory and Social Structure* (Glencoe, Ill.: The Free Press, 1957), p. 436.
31. *Ibid.*, p. 423.

32. *A New English Dictionary of Historical Principles,* James A. H. Murray, ed. (London, Oxford-Clarendon Press, 1888–1928).
33. *Webster's New World Dictionary of the American Language,* encycl. ed. (New York and Cleveland: World Publishing Company, 1951).
34. See unpublished paper by Nehemiah Jordan, "What Is Panic?," p. 8.
35. *Ibid.,* p. 7.
36. *Ibid.,* p. 12.
37. Murphy, pp. 988–989.
38. Lewis R. Wolberg, "Hypnosis in Medicine," *Bulletin of the New York Academy of Medicine,* Vol. 40, Feb. 1964, p. 107.
39. Jordan, p. 9.
40. Wolberg, p. 103; and William J. Bryan, *Legal Aspects of Hypnosis* (Springfield, Illinois: Charles C. Thomas, 1962), pp. 160–161. Compare footnote 44.
41. Wolberg, p. 103.
42. Herbert Spiegel, "Hypnosis and Invasion of Privacy," in *How to Defend a Criminal Case—From Arrest to Verdict,* Verne Lawyer and B. James George, Jr., eds. (Boston: American Trial Lawyers Association, 1967), p. 364.
43. *Ibid.,* pp. 357–358.
44. Compare Bryan, p. 161, Spiegel, p. 357, and Ernest R. Hilgard, "The Motivational Relevance of Hypnosis," in *Nebraska Symposium on Motivation,* David Levine, ed. (Lincoln: University of Nebraska Press, 1964), p. 20.
45. Examples can be found in experiments by Wolberg, pp. 105–107.
46. Bryan, pp. 249–255. See also Jack W. Brehm and Arthur R. Cohn, *Explorations in Cognitive Dissonance* (New York: John Wiley, 1962), pp. 286–288.
47. See discussion of research by Arthur R. Cohen (pp. 64–66 *supra*) and Blau (*supra*).
48. Hans H. Toch and Albert H. Hastorf, "Homeostasis in Psychology, a Review and Critique," *Psychiatry: Journal for the Study of Interpersonal Processes,* Vol. 18, No. 1, Feb. 1955, pp. 81–91.
49. Everett W. Bovard, "The Effects of Social Stimuli on the Response to Stress," in Hollander and Hunt, pp. 71–79.
50. David Krech and Richard S. Crutchfield, *Elements of Psychology* (New York: Alfred A. Knopf, 1958), p. 338.

51. Bernard Berelson and Gary A. Steiner, *Human Behavior—An Inventory of Scientific Findings* (New York: Harcourt, Brace, and World, Inc., 1964), pp. 249–252.
52. Hilgard, p. 19.
53. Hadley Cantril and Charles H. Bumstead, *Reflections on the Human Venture* (New York: New York University Press, 1960), p. 83.
54. S. I. Hayakawa, "Meaning, Symbols and Levels of Abstraction," in *Readings in Social Psychology*, T. M. Newcomb and E. L. Hartley, eds. (New York: Henry Holt and Co., 1947), pp. 190–203.
55. R. Stagner, *Psychology of Industrial Conflict* (New York: John Wiley, 1956), cited by Ralph M. Stogdill, *Individual Behavior and Group Achievement* (New York: Oxford University Press, 1959), p. 250.
56. Fritz Heider, *The Psychology of Interpersonal Relations* (New York: John Wiley and Sons, 1958), p. 112. [emphasis added]
57. S. E. Asch, "Effects of Group Pressures Upon the Modification and Distortion of Judgments," in *Group Dynamics*, Dorwin Cartwright and Alvin Zander, eds., 2nd ed. (Evanston, Ill.: Row, Peterson and Company, 1960), p. 189; Alberta Engvall Siegel and Sidney Siegel, "Reference Groups, Membership Groups, and Attitude Change," in Cartwright and Zander, p. 232.
58. Muzafer Sherif, *The Psychology of Social Norms* (New York: Harper and Brothers, 1936), p. 96; see also p. 108.
59. *Ibid.*, p. 111.
60. Leo Tolstoy, "The Death of Ivan Ilych," in *Tellers of Tales*, W. Somerset Maugham, ed. (New York: Doubleday and Company, 1939), pp. 590, 593.
61. Asch, p. 189.
62. Leon Festinger, *A Theory of Cognitive Dissonance* (Evanston, Ill.: Row, Peterson and Company, 1957), pp. 198–200.
63. Robert K. Merton, "Discrimination and the American Creed," in *Discrimination and National Welfare*, R. M. MacIver, ed. (New York: Harper & Row, Publishers, 1949), pp. 110, 111.
64. W. J. McKeachie, "Individual Conformity to Attitudes of Classroom Groups," *Journal of Abnormal and Social Psychology*, Vol. 48, 1953, pp. 401–409.
65. The effect of group standards and individual behavior in industry has been well documented by Chris Argyris in *Personality and Organization* (New York: Harper and Bros., 1957); see also

Rensis Likert, *New Patterns of Management* (New York: McGraw-Hill Book Company, 1961); and William F. Whyte, *Men at Work* (Homewood, Ill.: Dorsey, 1961).

66. Argyris, p. 230.
67. Murphy, pp. 277, 278.
68. Hannah Arendt, *Eichmann in Jerusalem: A Report on the Banality of Evil* (New York: Viking, 1963), p. 120; cited in Dolores Barracano Schmidt and Earl Robert Schmidt, *The Deputy Leader: Studies in Moral Responsibility* (Chicago: Scott, Forman, 1965), p. 125.
69. Examination of Joseph Kramer, Case I of the Trials of War Criminals entitled *U.S. vs. Brandt, et al.*, p. 1172; cited in Schmidt and Schmidt, p. 129.
70. Bruno Bettelheim, *The Informed Heart*, (Glencoe, Ill: Free Press, 1961), p. 45.
71. *Ibid.*, p. 86.
72. *Ibid.*, p. 102.
73. *Ibid.*, p. 128.
74. *Ibid.*, p. 261.
75. Robert H. Jackson, *Trial of War Criminals*, Documents, U.S. Gov. Printing Office, Wash., 1945, p. 4.
76. Jackson, Robert H. *Trial of German War Criminals*, Opening Address, U.S. Gov. Printing Office, 1946, p. 37.
77. *Ibid.*, p. 4.
78. Yoram Dinstein, *The Defence of "Obedience to Superior Orders" in International Law* (Leyden: A. W. Sijthoff, 1965), p. 65.
79. Bettelheim, p. 45.
80. *Ibid.*, p. 70.
81. Murray Horwitz, "Psychological Needs as a Function of Social Environments," in *The State of the Social Sciences*, Leonard D. White, ed. (Chicago: University of Chicago Press, 1956), pp. 174, 167.
82. *Ibid.*, p. 167.
83. Morton Deutsch, "The Interpretation of Praise and Criticism as a Function of Their Social Context," *Journal of Abnormal and Social Psychology*, Vol. 62, No. 2, 1961, pp. 391–400.
84. William Bradford Huie, *Three Lives for Mississippi* (New York: WCC Books, 1965).
85. Oliver Wendell Holmes, Jr., *The Common Law* (Boston: Little, Brown and Company, 1881), p. 54.
86. *Ibid.*, p. 55; see also pp. 52–53, cited pp. 9–10.

87. Aubrey Menen, *The Prevalence of Witches* (New York: Charles Scribner's Sons, 1953).
88. Holmes, p. 54.
89. See pages 84–88, *supra.*
90. J. W. Atkinson, "The Achievement Motive and Recall of Interrupted and Completed Tasks," *Journal of Experimental Psychology,* Vol. 46, 1953, pp. 381–390, cited in Ernest R. Hilgard, *Introduction to Psychology,* 2nd ed. (New York: Harcourt, Brace & World, 1957), p. 297. See also B. Zeigarnik, "Das Behalten erledigter und unerledigter Handlungen," *Psychologische Forschung,* 1927, Vol. 9, pp. 1–85; Murray Horwitz, "The Recall of Interrupted Group Tasks: An Experimental Study of Individual Motivation in Relation to Group Goals," in Cartwright and Zander, p. 370.
91. *Nebraska Symposium on Motivation,* Marshall R. Jones, ed. (Lincoln: University of Nebraska Press, 1956), p. 168.
92. *Director of Public Prosecution v. Smith,* 3 W.L.R. 546 (1960), 3 All E.R. 161 (1960), 44 Cr. App. R. 261.
93. *Regina v. Smyth,* 98 C.L.R. 163 (1957).
94. J. L. Travers and Norval Morris, "Imputed Intent in Murder, or Smith v. Smyth," *The Australian Law Journal,* Vol. 35, Aug. 31, 1961, p. 154.
95. *Ibid.,* p. 156.
96. *Ibid.,* p. 157. [emphasis added]
97. *Ibid.,* p. 155.
98. *Ibid.,* pp. 156–157.
99. *Ibid.,* p. 161.
100. Leon Green, "Foreseeability in Negligence Law," in *The Litigation Process in Tort Law* (Indianapolis: Bobbs-Merrill, 1965), pp. 305; see also pp. 302–303.
101. William J. Brennan, Jr., "Law and Psychiatry Must Join in Defending Mentally Ill Criminals," *American Bar Association Journal,* Vol. 49, No. 3, March 1963, p. 239.
102. *Ibid.,* p. 240.
103. Martin Buber, *I and Thou,* 2nd ed. (New York: Charles Scribner's Sons, 1958), p. 13.
104. Sheldon Glueck, *Law and Psychiatry, Cold War or Entente Cordiale?* (Baltimore: The Johns Hopkins University Press, 1962), pp. 58–59.
105. The Committee on Psychiatry and Law of the Group for the

Advancement of Psychiatry, "Criminal Responsibility and Psychiatric Expert Testimony," Rep. No. 26, Topeka, Kansas, May 1954, p. 4.

106. *Ibid.*, p. 5.
107. *Interim Report of the State of New York Temporary Commission on Revision of the Penal Law and Criminal Code,* Legislative Documents, Vol. 8, 1963, p. 19.
108. Ronald Leifer, "The Psychiatrist and Tests of Criminal Responsibility," *American Psychologist,* Vol. 19, No. 11 (Nov. 1964), p. 825.
109. *Durham v. United States,* 214 F.2d 862 (1954); and see *State v. Jones,* 50 N.H. 369, p. 394 (1871); A.L.R. Ann. 2d Vol. 45, pp. 1447–1466; and see Travers and Morris.
110. See *Smith v. United States,* 36 F.2d 548, pp. 549, 550 (1929).
111. 214 F.2d at p. 874.
112. Leifer, p. 828.
113. Compare Revised New York Penal Law §30.05 and the Commission Staff Comments in *McKinney's Consolidated Laws of New York Annotated,* (Brooklyn, N.Y.: Edward Thompson Company, 1965), pp. 14 and 257. See also *United States v. Freeman,* 357 F.2d 606 (2nd Circuit, 1966).
114. Compare *Interim Report of the New York State Temporary Commission,* pp. 21–22.
115. Frederick Pollock and Frederic William Maitland, *The History of English Law,* Vol. II (Cambridge: Cambridge University Press, 1962), pp. 474–475.

CHAPTER IV

1. *Morissette v. United States,* 342 U.S. 246, 264 (1951).
2. *The Concise Oxford Dictionary of Current English,* 5th ed. (New York: Oxford University Press, 1914).
3. N. M. Korkunov, *General Theory of Law,* trans. by W. G. Hastings (Boston: The Boston Book Company, 1909), p. 59; Deuteronomy 30:15–19, *The Holy Scriptures According to the Masoretic Text* (Philadelphia: Jewish Publication Society, 1955), p. 278; *The Nicomachean Ethics of Aristotle,* J. E. C. Welldon, trans. (London: Macmillan Co., 1934), Book III, Chapters 5–7, pp. 69–76.

4. *Model Penal Code* (Philadelphia: American Law Institute, 1962), §§2.01, 2.08, 4.01.
5. *Beverley's Case*, 76 Eng. Rep., K.B. 1603, pp. 1118, 1123.
6. Raymond G. McCarthy, "Alcoholism: Attitudes and Attacks, 1775–1935," in *Understanding Alcoholism, The Annals, American Academy of Political and Social Sciences*, Vol. 315, January 1958, pp. 15–16.
7. Julius Isaacs, "Legislation and Alcoholism," *Public Health Report*, U.S. Department of Health, Education and Welfare, Vol. 70, No. 12, 1955, pp. 1161, 1164.
8. Carl Rubington, "The Chronic Drunkenness Offender," in *Understanding Alcoholism*, pp. 65, 66.
9. *Heideman v. United States*, 259 F.2d 943, p. 946 (1958). See also *Hopt v. People*, 104 U.S. 631 (1882).
10. *Model Penal Code*, §2.08(4); and see Revised Penal Law of New York, §15.25.
11. Jonas B. Robitscher, "Pursuit of Agreement," in *Psychiatry and the Law* (Philadelphia: Lippincott, 1966), pp. 186–187. Constitutionality of taking a blood test without the defendant's consent was upheld in *Schmerber v. California*, 384 U.S. 757 (1966), and *Breithaupt v. Abram*, 352 U.S. 432 (1957).
12. Leon A. Greenberg, "Intoxication and Alcoholism: Physiological Factors," in *Understanding Alcoholism*, pp. 22, 28.
13. Robitscher, p. 184.
14. *Ibid.*, p. 180.
15. Donald Horton, "The Functions of Alcohol in Primitive Societies," in *Personality in Nature, Society, and Culture*, Clyde Kluckhohn and Henry A. Murray, eds. (New York: Alfred A. Knopf, 1949), pp. 540 *et seq.*
16. *Ibid.*, p. 541.
17. *Ibid.*, p. 546.
18. Robitscher, p. 184.
19. Greenberg, pp. 26, 27.
20. Robitscher, p. 188.
21. *Ibid.*, p. 189.
22. Stanley Schachter and Bibb Latané, "Crime Cognition and Autonomic Nervous System," in *Nebraska Symposium on Motivation, 1964*, David Levine, ed. (Lincoln: University of Nebraska Press, 1964), pp. 221–273.
23. *Ibid.*, pp. 223–231.

24. Hervey Cleckley, *The Mask of Sanity*, 2nd ed. (St. Louis: C. V. Mosby Co., 1950); cited in David T. Lykken, "A Study of Anxiety in the Sociopathic Personality," *Journal of Abnormal and Social Psychology*, Vol. 55, No. 1, July, 1957, p. 6.
25. Lykken, pp. 6–10.
26. Schachter and Latané, pp. 235 *et seq.*
27. *Ibid.*, p. 236.
28. *Ibid.*, p. 245.
29. *Ibid.*, pp. 242–243.
30. *Ibid.*, pp. 251–252.
31. *Ibid.*, pp. 266, 267.
32. *Ibid.*, pp. 271, 272. And see the description of sociopathic murderers in Truman Capote, *In Cold Blood* (New York: Random House, 1965), pp. 398–401 and 310–317.
33. Joseph Statten, Karl Menninger, Irwin Rosen, and Martin Mayman, "Murder Without Apparent Motive: A Study in Personality Disorganization," *American Journal of Psychiatry*, Vol. 117, 1960, pp. 48–53, 51, 52.
34. See *Robinson v. California*, 370 U.S. 660, p. 667 (1962); *Driver v. Hinnant*, 356 F.2d 761, p. 764 (1966); and *Easter v. District of Columbia*, 361 F.2d 50, p. 53 (1966).

CHAPTER V

1. *Black's Law Dictionary*, 4th ed. (St. Paul, Minnesota: West Publishing Company, 1951), pp. 917 and 309; *Webster's New World Dictionary of the American Language*, encycl. ed., Vol. I (Cleveland and New York: The World Publishing Company, 1951), p. 746.
2. S. I. Hayakawa, "Meaning, Symbols, and Levels of Abstraction," in *Readings in Social Psychology*, T. M. Newcomb and E. L. Hartley, eds. (New York: Holt, Rinehart and Winston, 1947), p. 199.
3. *Morissette v. United States*, 342 U.S. 246 (1951).
4. Fritz Heider, *The Psychology of Interpersonal Relations* (New York: John Wiley and Sons, 1958), p. 110.
5. Ralph M. Stogdill, *Individual Behavior and Group Achievement* (New York: Oxford University Press, 1959), p. 128.

6. Oliver Wendell Holmes, Jr., *The Common Law* (Boston: Little, Brown and Company, 1881), p. 54.
7. Franz Alexander and Hugo Staub, *The Criminal, the Judge, and the Public,* rev. ed. (New York: Collier Books, 1962), p. 98.
8. Holmes, p. 54.
9. Rudolf Von Ihering, *Law as a Means to an End* (Boston: The Boston Book Company, 1913), pp. 8–9.
10. Heider, p. 100.
11. A. A. Brill, trans. and ed., *The Basic Writings of Sigmund Freud* (New York: The Modern Library, 1938), p. 96.
12. *Ibid.*, p. 106.
13. Hadley Cantril and Charles H. Bumstead, *Reflections on the Human Venture* (New York: New York University Press, 1960), p. 84.
14. Holmes, p. 52.
15. Heider, p. 94.
16. *Ibid.*, pp. 112–114.
17. *Ibid.*, p. 112.
18. *Ibid.*, p. 113.
19. Sol Kugelmass, Shlomo Breznitz, and Tamar Breznitz, "The Development of Intentionality in Moral Judgment, Suggestions and Initial Test," in *Studies in Psychology*, Rivka R. Eifermann, ed., Scripta Hierosolymitana, XIV (Jerusalem: Magnes Press, 1965), pp. 82, 45–96; and Shlomo Breznitz and Sol Kugelmass, "Intentionality and Moral Judgment: Development Stages," to be published in *Child Development.* Compare Jean Piaget, *The Moral Judgment of the Child* (New York: Harcourt, Brace and World, 1932).
20. See James Marshall, *Law and Psychology in Conflict* (Indianapolis: Bobbs-Merrill, 1966), p. 50.
21. Heider, pp. 109–110.
22. *Ibid.*, p. 110.
23. See William F. Whyte, *Street Corner Society* (Chicago: University of Chicago Press, 1943), p. 24.
24. Heider, p. 116.
25. *Ibid.*, p. 114.
26. Compare Murder with Manslaughter, *Model Penal Code,* §§210.2(1) and 210.3(1).
27. David R. Miller and Guy E. Swanson, "The Study of Conflict," in *Nebraska Symposium on Motivation*, 1956, Marshall R. Jones,

ed. (Lincoln: University of Nebraska Press, 1956), pp. 146, 157–158.

28. *Knierim v. Izzo,* 22 Ill. 2d 73, 174 N.W. 2d 157 (1961); *Battala v. State,* 10 N.Y. 2d 337, 176 N.E. 729 (1961), and see "Torts: Intentional Infliction of Mental Suffering," 11 *DePaul Law Review,* Vol. 11, 1961, p. 151, and "Intentional Infliction of Mental Distress," *Brooklyn Law Review,* Vol. 28, 1962, p. 354.
29. Harry Kalven, Jr., and Hans Zeisel, *The American Jury* (Boston: Little, Brown and Company, 1966), pp. 385, 382.
30. *Rex v. Thompson,* A.C. 221, 235 (1918).
31. Rule 311 of the *Model Code of Evidence* (Philadelphia: American Law Institute, 1942); see also Glanville Williams, *The Proof of Guilt,* 3rd ed. (London: Stevens and Sons, 1963), p. 237.
32. Irving Sarnoff, "Psychoanalytic Theory and Social Attitudes," *The Public Opinion Quarterly,* Vol. 24, 1960, p. 152.
33. Heider, p. 120.
34. *Ibid.*
35. Herbert M. Jenkins and William C. Ward, "Judgment of Contingency Between Responses and Outcomes," *Psychological Monographs: General and Applied,* Vol. 79, No. 1, pp. 1–17.
36. John Henry Wigmore, *A Treatise on the Anglo-American System of Evidence in Trial at Common Law,* Vol. I, 2nd ed. (Boston: Little, Brown and Company, 1923), §302.
37. Compare *Model Penal Code,* §4.01(2).
38. Edward Kasner and James Newman, *Mathematics and the Imagination* (New York: Simon and Schuster, 1940), p. 226.
39. *Ibid.,* p. 229.
40. Hans H. Toch and Richard Schulte, "Readiness to Perceive Violence as a Result of Police Training," *British Journal of Psychology,* Vol. 52, No. 4, 1961, pp. 389–393.
41. Gardner Murphy, *Personality* (New York, Harper and Row, 1947), pp. 285–286.
42. *Ibid.,* p. 272.
43. Patricia Waly and Stuart W. Cook, "Effects of Attitudes on Judgments of Plausibility," *Journal of Personality and Social Psychology,* 1965, Vol. 2, No. 5, pp. 745–749.
44. Gordon W. Allport and Leo Postman, *The Psychology of Rumor* (New York: Henry Holt and Company, 1947).
45. Benjamin Cardozo, *The Nature of the Judicial Process* (New Haven: Yale University Press, 1921), pp. 167–168.

46. See Marshall, Chapter II.
47. Lawrence S. Kubie, "Implications for Legal Procedure of the Fallibility of Human Memory," *Pennsylvania Law Review,* Vol. 108, 1959, pp. 108, 159.
48. *Ibid.,* p. 67.
49. Francis A. Allen, "Criminal Law," in symposium, "Mr. Justice Holmes: Some Modern Views," *Chicago Law Review,* Vol. 31, 1964, pp. 257, 262.
50. Wendell Johnson, *People in Quandaries* (New York: Harper & Row, Publishers, 1946), p. ix.
51. Alexander and Staub, p. 40.
52. Charles A. Beard, *The Republic* (New York: The Viking Press, 1943), p. 88.
53. Williams, p. 222.
54. Kalven and Zeisel, p. 337.

CHAPTER VI

1. Fritz Heider, *The Psychology of Interpersonal Relations* (New York: John Wiley and Sons, 1958), p. 110.
2. James A. H. Murray, *A New English Dictionary of Historical Principles* (London: Oxford University Press, 1888–1928).
3. Samuel Williston, *Treatise on the Law of Contracts,* 3rd ed. (Mt. Kisco, New York: Baker, Voorhis, 1957), §94, p. 338.
4. *Ibid.,* p. 339.
5. Oliver Wendell Holmes, Jr., *The Common Law* (Boston: Little, Brown and Company, 1881), p. 303.
6. See also *Benjamin Foster Co. v. Commonwealth,* 318 Mass. 190, 196, 61 N.E.2d 147, 150–151, (1945). And see Charles E. Osgood, "On the Nature of Meaning," in *Current Perspectives in Social Psychology,* E. P. Hollander and Raymond G. Hunt, eds. (New York: Oxford University Press, 1963), pp. 233, 235, 236.
7. Benjamin Cardozo, *The Nature of the Judicial Process* (New Haven: Yale University Press, 1921), pp. 170–171.
8. *Baines v. Woodfall,* 6 C.B. (n.s.) 657, 677, 141 Eng. Rep. 613, 617 (1859).
9. See Francis J. DiVesta, Donald L. Meyer, and Judson Mills,

"Confidence in an Expert as a Function of His Judgments," *Human Relations*, Vol. 17, No. 3, 1964, p. 235.

10. Lenore G. Marshall, "Latest Will," *The American Scholar* (Spring, 1965), p. 255, copyright *The American Scholar*, reprinted by permission.
11. Rudolf Von Ihering, *Law as a Means to an End* (Boston: The Boston Book Company, 1913), p. 74.
12. C. K. Ogden and I. A. Richards, *The Meaning of Meaning*, 8th ed. (New York: Harcourt, Brace, and Co., 1946), p. 194.
13. William F. Young, Jr., "Equivocation in the Making of Agreements," *Columbia Law Review*, Vol. 64, 1964, p. 619.
14. See *Morissette v. United States*, 342 U.S. 246 (1951); *Holy Trinity Church v. United States*, 143 U.S. 457, p. 465 (1892); *The State of Rhode Island v. The State of Massachusetts*, 12 Peters 657, p. 722 (1838); *Slaughter-House Cases*, 83 U.S. 394, p. 407 (1872); and *Pennoyer v. McConnaughy*, 140 U.S. 1, p. 23 (1890).
15. Walter F. Dodd, *Cases on Constitutional Law* (St. Paul, Minn.: West Publishing Company, 1942), p. 52.
16. Morris R. Cohen, *American Thought: A Critical Sketch* (Glencoe, Ill.: The Free Press, 1954), p. 162.
17. *McBoyle v. United States*, 283 U.S. 25, p. 27 (1930).
18. Dodd, p. 54, sermon preached in 1717, quoted in John C. Gray, *The Nature and Sources of the Law*, 2nd ed. (New York: The Macmillan Co., 1921), p. 125.
19. Heider, p. 235.

CHAPTER VII

1. James Marshall, *Swords and Symbols: The Technique of Sovereignty* (New York: Oxford University Press, 1939), p. 55.
2. Melville J. Herskovits, *Man and His Works: The Science of Cultural Anthropology* (New York: Alfred A. Knopf, 1948), p. 345.
3. A. E. Housman, *Last Poems* (New York: Holt, Rinehart and Winston, 1922), p. 29.
4. Benjamin Cardozo, *The Paradoxes of Legal Science* (New York: Columbia University Press, 1928), p. 11.
5. See *Bayly v. Merrel*, Cro. Jac. 387 (1616).

6. *Brown v. The Board of Education*, 347 U.S. 483 (1954).
7. *Ibid.*, pp. 492–493.
8. James Marshall, *Law and Psychology in Conflict* (Indianapolis: Bobbs-Merrill, 1966), Chaps. I and III.
9. Henry H. Foster, Jr., "Divorce Reform," *Bar Bulletin*, New York County Lawyers Association, Vol. 4, No. 22, 1964–1965, pp. 165–173.
10. See Herskovits, p. 331.
11. Harry Kalven, Jr., and Hans Zeisel, *The American Jury* (Boston: Little, Brown and Company, 1966), p. 340.
12. *Ibid.*, pp. 339–340.
13. Ronald Leifer, "The Psychiatrist and Tests of Criminal Responsibility," *American Psychologist*, Vol. 19, No. 11, Nov. 1964, pp. 828–829.
14. Erich Fromm, *Man for Himself* (New York: Holt, Rinehart and Winston, 1947), p. 236.
15. Franz Alexander and Hugo Staub, *The Criminal, the Judge, and the Public*, rev. ed. (New York: Collier Books, 1962), p. 146; see also Jackson Toby, "Criminal Motivation," *British Journal of Criminology*, Vol. 2, No. 4, 1962, p. 324.
16. Sheldon Glueck, *Law and Psychiatry, Cold War or Entente Cordiale?* (Baltimore: Johns Hopkins University Press, 1962), pp. 9–10.
17. See *supra*, pp. 79, 119–120.
18. Leifer, p. 830.
19. Fromm, p. 235.
20. George Meredith, *Diana of the Crossways* (New York: Charles Scribner's Sons, 1916), p. 99.
21. Gerhard O. W. Mueller, "The Public Law of Wrongs—Its Concepts in the World of Reality," in "Fundamental Concepts of Public Law Symposium," No. 2, *Journal of Public Law*, Vol. 10, No. 2 (1962), pp. 237–238.
22. *New York Times Co. v. Sullivan*, 376 U.S. 272, pp. 279–280 (1964); approved in *Curtis Publishing Co. v. Butts*, 388 U.S. 130, p. 134 (1967).
23. *Williams v. New York*, 337 U.S. 241 (1948).
24. See U.S.C.A., Amend. 1–5 (1961), 434–435 and Cum. Supp.
25. *People v. Dusablon*, 16 N.Y. 2d 9, 261 N.Y. Supp. 2d 38 (1965).
26. *State v. Lucas*, 152 A.2d 50, p. 74 (New Jersey, 1959); *People v. Moseley*, 20 N.Y. 2nd 64 (1967).

27. *State v. Lucas*, p. 75.
28. Harold D. Lasswell and Richard C. Donnelly, "The Continuing Debate Over Responsibility: An Introduction to Isolating the Condemnation Sanction," *Yale Law Journal*, Vol. 68, 1959, pp. 881–891.
29. Sam J. Ervin, Senator, "Uncompensated Counsel: They Do Not Meet the Constitutional Mandate," *American Bar Association Journal*, Vol. 49, No. 5, May 1964, p. 438.
30. Karl Menninger and Joseph Statten, "What Psychiatry Proposes for Offenders," *Menninger Quarterly*, Vol. 15, No. 3, Fall 1961, p. 9.
31. Cited by William J. Brennan, Jr., "Law and Psychiatry Must Join in Defending Mentally Ill Criminals," *American Bar Association Journal*, Vol. 49, No. 3, March 1963, p. 240.
32. Ross Stagner, "Limitations on Punishment," *Journal of Abnormal and Social Psychology*, Vol. 38, No. 2, 1943, p. 186.
33. W. A. Bowes, *The Romance of the Law Merchant* (London: Sweet and Maxwell, 1923).
34. Wendell Johnson, *People in Quandaries* (New York: Harper & Row, Publishers, 1946), p. 17.
35. Claude Bernard, *An Introduction to the Study of Experimental Medicine*, English ed. (New York: The Macmillan Company, 1927), p. 40.

Index